DATE DUE			

MUSICAL INTERPRETATION

MUSICAL

INTERPRETATION

ITS LAWS AND PRINCIPLES, AND THEIR APPLICATION IN

TEACHING AND PERFORMING

BY

TOBIAS MATTHAY

(PROFESSOR, LECTURER AND FELLOW OF THE ROYAL ACADEMY OF MUSIC,
LONDON, AUTHOR OF "THE ACT OF TOUCH," "FIRST PRIN-
CIPLES," "SOME COMMENTARIES ON PIANO PLAYING,"
"RELAXATION STUDIES," "THE CHILD'S FIRST
STEPS," "THE ROTATION ELEMENT," ETC.
FOUNDER OF THE TOBIAS MATTHAY
PIANOFORTE SCHOOL, LONDON.)

GREENWOOD PRESS, PUBLISHERS
WESTPORT, CONNECTICUT

Originally published in 1913 by Joseph Williams, Ltd.,
London and The Boston Music Co., Boston

Reprinted by Greenwood Press, Inc.

First Greenwood reprinting 1970
Second Greenwood reprinting 1977

Library of Congress catalog card number 72-109787
ISBN 0-8371-4277-6

Printed in the United States of America

PREFACE

FOR many years past I have been urged to put into a permanent and available form my enunciation of those Principles and Laws of Interpretation, knowledge of which has proved to be one of the main causes of the success of the army of teachers who have arisen from my school.

The first step towards this end was the preparation, in the year 1909, of a set of Lectures covering this ground. These I condensed later into a single lecture, and this was first delivered publicly in Manchester to Dr. Carroll's Association of Teachers during the season of 1909–10. Subsequently, it was repeated to the Edinburgh Musical Education Society, to the London Music Teachers' Association (in 1910) and its Branches; it was also given at the Royal Academy of Music in the same year, and at my own School, and elsewhere.

A full synopsis also appeared in the "Music Student" of April, 1910, and elsewhere. I, nevertheless, still delayed issuing the material in book form, as I felt, in view of the extreme importance of the matters dealt with, that I would like to expand it, but lack of time has prevented my doing so.

As, however, some of our more up-to-date theorists are now doing me the honour to apply, in their recent works, some of the ideas first enunciated in these lectures of mine (and in my "First Principles," 1905, and "Act of Touch," 1903) such, for instance, as the vital one of recognizing in *Progression* or *Movement* the actual basis of all Rhythm and Shape in Music, I feel compelled to issue these lectures now as originally delivered. Additional matter is given in the form of Notes; and I leave for later on, perhaps, the issue of a Supplement giving further details and illustrative Examples.

It will be found, that while this work deals with the subject mainly from the pianist's point of view, nevertheless most of the principles here formulated apply with equal force to all other forms of musical performance. Many of the same laws of Interpretation which apply to Pianoforte playing also hold good whether we are players of stringed instruments or wind instruments, or are vocalists or organ-players or conductors. We cannot play even on a penny whistle without coming under the sway of such laws! Hence I hope that this little volume may prove helpful to all music-teachers and would-be performers, artists as well as students, whatever their specialty.[1]

Some of the main points here dealt with are: (a) the difference between letting a pupil shift for himself and helping him to learn; (b) the difference between mere cramming and real teaching; (c) the difference between merely making a pupil "do things" and teaching him to think — to the end that he may know what to do, why to do it, and how to do it; (d) the exposition of the true nature of Rhythm and Shape in Music — as Progression or Movement towards definite landmarks; (e) the true nature of Rubato in all its forms, small and large, simple and compound, and the laws of its application; (f) consideration of the element of Duration, and, allied to this, rules as to the application of the damper-pedal; also, rules as to the application of Tone-variety, Fingering, Memorizing, etc., and some speculations as to the ultimate reason of the power that Music has over us.

To prevent misunderstanding, I must at once state that

[1] Helpful even to the operators of mechanical pianos.

I do not claim that artists are "made" by the mere enunciation and teaching of such laws and principles as here given, or by those of instrumental technique — although no success can be attained without obedience to these same laws and principles. No, the really great artist always has been, is now, and ever will be, a most rare phenomenon. His advent depends on so many things uniting in one single individual — the highest gifts of imagination and invention, therefore high mental powers (yes, the really great artist must also have high reasoning power), physical and mental endurance, extreme enthusiasm for his chosen art, good health, and the *opportunities* to require the requisite skill *to work in strict obedience to the laws of his art.*

Hence it is not claimed that the truthful Analysis and Synthesis of art or its technique can transform dullards into poets and seers, but what *has been amply proven* is, that such teachings do inevitably help the ordinary student to succeed in attaining to far higher ideals than he could have reached without such help, and that the "heaven-born" Genius (when he does appear) has many years of useful life added to his career, years otherwise wasted in futile experiments, while his path towards still higher perfections is thus rendered possible and easy — and his appreciation of truth in art made more sound. Such teaching therefore makes for Progress, not only in Music but in Life itself.

In thanking the many who have encouraged me to undertake the publication of this little work, I must also again thank Mrs. Kennedy-Fraser, of Edinburgh, for her invaluable help with my proofs.

TOBIAS MATTHAY.

HASLEMERE, September, 1912.

CONTENTS

SECTION I

INTRODUCTORY

ix

SECTION II

The Nature of Musical Attention and of Musical Shape

SECTION III

The Element of Rubato

CONTENTS

SECTION IV

CONCERNING CERTAIN DETAILS IN THE APPLICATION OF TONE-INFLECTION
AND THE BEARING OF TOUCH-TEACHING AND FINGERING, ETC., ON
INTERPRETATION

SECTION V

As to Pedalling and the Element of Duration

CONTENTS

SECTION VI

THE PURPOSE OF ART-EXPRESSION AND ITS RELATION TO THE INFINITE

MUSICAL
INTERPRETATION

SECTION I

INTRODUCTORY

SOME GENERAL PRINCIPLES OF TEACHING AND LEARNING

THE teaching of Interpretation is so complex a problem that at a first glance it seems hopeless to try to cover the ground in one or two short lectures. All one can do is to select some few of the more salient points, points in regard to which the young teacher or performer (and often the older one) is most apt to fail. This then, is what I propose doing, it being understood that no attempt is here made to treat the subject exhaustively.

The main points I have selected are:

(1) The difference between Practice and mere Strumming.

(2) The difference between Teaching and Cramming.

(3) How one's mind can be brought to bear upon one's work.

(4) Correct ideas of Time and Shape.

(5) The element of Rubato and its application.

(6) The elements of Duration and Pedalling and their application.

(7) Incidentally, some details as to the application of the element of Tone-variety.

1

General attitude of teacher.

It is impossible, however, to make clear even these particular essentials of teaching, without first taking a cursory glance *at the whole problem* — the *general attitude* of the teacher towards those he wishes to help.   To begin with, let us recognise the fact, that, accurately speaking, we cannot "teach" anyone anything — in the sense of our being able *directly to lodge* any knowledge of ours in another mind.

The learner can only be helped to learn.

All we cán really do is to stimulate another mind *to wish to learn*, and suggestively to place before that other mind the things which it is desirable should be apprehended.   It is always the other mind which has to make the effort to apprehend, and unless that effort *is* made nothing can be learnt.

We cannot teach others, but we *can help them* to learn. In fact, I will go so far as to say that unless we teachers do recognise this fundamental truth, we cannot hope to begin to succeed in our vocation.   We shall also see that one of the very points I wish to insist upon is closely allied to this truth.   Let me at once state it here:

The first law of teaching.

Good teaching consists not in trying to make the pupil *do things* so that the result of his efforts shall *seem* like playing, but consists in trying to make him *think*, so that it shall *really* be playing.

The good teacher does not try to turn his pupil into an automaton, but tries to prompt him to grow into a living, intelligent being.   But more of this anon.[1]

---

[1] As I shall explain later, the fallacious attitude is to endeavour to use *our* will and intelligence so that the doings of our pupil's fingers may sound plausible, whereas the correct attitude is to use our intelligence so that the pupil will all the time use *his* own intelligence and *his* own will, and may thus learn to guide his fingers correctly, alike musically, and technically.

Undoubtedly, one of the first things we have to combat in a pupil is the wish to be saved all trouble and effort, and to have the "learning" done by the teacher. Indeed, the ordinary pupil invariably starts with the notion, that all he has to do is to be passive and "receptive" — like a laboratory funnel with mouth widely gaping, ready to receive any chemicals (pleasant or otherwise) which the operating chemist may see fit to pour in. This attitude must be at once kindly but firmly combated, and the pupil must be made to see, that it is for *him* to try to learn, for him to try to apprehend and to assimilate those things to which the teacher is anxious to call his attention.

The most usual fault of the student.

Certainly, there are direct and there are indirect (or empirical) methods of teaching in all branches of education; and, as you know, I claim that my teaching-methods *are* direct — but we now see that this "directness" can refer solely *to the method of placing things* before a pupil.

The first general conclusion we are thus driven to accept is the need for purposeful brain-use, on the part of both teacher and pupil. With regard to the pupil, not only is brain-use (i.e. reasoning) imperative during lesson-time, it is even more imperative during the practice-hour when there is no help available from outside. How often indeed do we find the pupil's work brought back worse than at a preceding lesson, in spite of what would seem to have been most judiciously thought-out and carefully worded advice! And why is this so? Simply, because the pupil in the interval, instead of really practising, has tried with might and main to make himself (or herself) into an automatic *strumming-machine*. Yes, often it is the pupil's fault, he either will not, or cannot use his brains.

Both teacher and pupil must learn to think.

But believe me, far more often still, it is the teacher's fault, owing to his not having correctly *shown* the student *how* to use his brains during practice, or not having diplomatically enough insisted on real practice, in place of such mere gymnastic strumming.

How to practise.

The first thing to do then, is to give the pupil a clear idea of what does constitute real practice.[1]

The danger of automaticity.

Remember that the mistaken desideratum with which the student starts work is just this, it seems to him that the ideal state would be to be able to do *without thinking*. Often enough he does try his utmost to exercise his muscles in his pieces, his studies and techniques — and he does so, believing piano-playing to be a purely gymnastic pursuit like walking and running, etc. Even admitting the necessity for muscular automaticity, he does not realise that a certain amount of reflection is imperative in acquiring it; that walking, running, and breathing, purely automatic as they must be *in the end*, are all the better for a little reflection on the right ways of doing them.[2]

The average student then, if left to himself, will assuredly try to make himself into a mere automaton in his practice-hour, from sheer horror of the discomfort and irksomeness of *mental* effort.

Therefore, this is the first and ever-present obstacle with which we teachers have to contend. We must be prepared to drive home to the pupil that the thing *most to be avoided* is this very automaticity which seems so attractive to him,

[1] Realise, that the average student has a fixed idea that Piano-practice is a purely gymnastic exercise — he lives in the hope that by going over the ground often enough, the piece may at last "do itself" *without his thinking about it at all* — a mere exercising therefore of the muscles concerned.

[2] Even the athlete must use his judgement, and those who are too lazy or decadent to do their athletics personally must still give their minds to the exhibited exercise, if they mean to derive any interest from it.

and into which his natural bent will only too assuredly lead him. We may use persuasion or threats, coaxing or snarling, sledge hammer or velvet paw upon him, but if any good work is to be done, we must in some way or other bring him to avoid automatic practice.

Really, there is nothing more fatal for our musical sense, than to allow ourselves — by the hour — to *hear* musical sounds without really *listening* to them; and this holds true whether the sounds are made by ourselves or by others; for unless we do listen *attentively*, we are at that moment inevitably forming habits of lax attention.[1] The danger of not really listening.

Here I must digress for a moment, to make plainer what is meant by "really listening," for we cannot get any further unless we are quite clear on this point. Let us, for instance, take a page of print or music. If we turn our eyes upon it, the light from the page pours in upon us, whether we attend to its meaning or not. We may realise that it is Listening defined.

---

[1] To sound the notes of a piece through as a mere physical exercise, is not only useless but positively harmful musically; and this applied as much to the practice of Studies and Techniques as to that of pieces, for in all repetitions we are always forming or fixing habits — musical ones and technical ones — and it behoves us therefore to see to it that good habits and not bad ones are being insisted upon — habits of keen attention, for instance, and not habits of laxity of attention. It must be constantly insisted upon, that if we try to make the piece, or study, or technical exercise "go by itself," this, so far from being "practice" is indeed the opposite — it is *un-practice*. For in trying to turn ourselves into human automata we are doing all we can to render it impossible for us to acquire those habits of mind — of attention — which enable us to play with success; and we shall, in the end, find our *head* listening merely to the doings of our *spine!* And this is no mere figure of speech, for it describes quite accurately what does occur in such cases; that is, we here have the conscious, *could-be* intelligent brain engaged in merely noticing (instead of directing) the clockwork doings of our spinal or ganglionic centres! Automatic practice, useless, even for techniques.

a page of print, we may even read it out aloud, but it conveys no definite meaning until we do bring our minds upon it. We derive no information from the constant stream of varied light-impressions pouring in through the iris *unless we analyse the impressions* made on our nerve-ends; unless we (consciously or unconsciously) investigate the impressions there received, we notice nothing, learn nothing, and do not really see *anything*.[1]

Precisely so is it with our ears, I might say it is even more so, for we cannot shut our physical ears as we can our eyes. All sounds that occur within earshot will certainly reach our ear-drums and the nerve-ends of the inner ear, whether we "listen" or not. But we may derive from this stream of sounds either a mere vague impression that *some sort* of sound is occurring, or we may, if we turn our minds upon the sound, discover definitely *what* it consists of and means.

We do not really see or hear unless we analyse. We may, even without attention, realise the fact that some music is being made, but we shall certainly not understand a note of it, unless we do purposely, all the time, notice and in fact *analyse* the stream of aural-impressions pouring in upon us.

[1] An excellent experiment is, to turn our eyes upon a window covered by a light, diaphanous, gauzy curtain. We shall find, while keeping our eyes quite stationary, that we can allow ourselves to become conscious *either* of the pattern of the curtain, or of the trees or other objects outside the window. True, a slight focussing adjustment of the iris-muscles occurs in this case, but the main, important fact taught us is, that we may either notice the curtain itself or the things beyond it at will. Which of the two we do thus observe depends upon the direction we give to our powers of mental-analysis. Moreover, the things we do not thus analyse we also do not observe — and this, although the light rays do pour in upon us all the time, both from the curtain and from the objects beyond it!

No one is quite so foolish as to try to write or draw without at least taking the trouble to *look* at the paper he is engaged upon. Nevertheless, most music-students fail to realise that it is just as idiotic to try to play any musical instrument without at least taking the trouble accurately to listen to it — all the time.[1]

Yes, that is where "Ear-training" comes in. But how much rubbish is written and talked in this cause — a most righteous cause, when really understood and not perverted into faddism. It would seem that many people imagine "Ear-training" to be a process of actually training a portion of one's brain (previously otherwise employed) to be impressed by sounds, or a training of the nerve-ends of the ear-organ itself! Or, perhaps even, a training of the skin and flesh itself — the lobes of the outer ear!

As to ear-training, good and bad.

[1] This is one of the greatest difficulties the teacher has to contend with. The average pupil does not in the least realise that he must bring his aural consciousness on the work in hand; neither will he take the trouble to judge what he should do, nor how he should do it, nor will he deign to listen to the *actual sounds* he is making. Yet when he writes his own name he takes care to "listen with his eyes" on the paper! And even with the best intention to listen and attend properly, the student is apt to fail. You must explain to him therefore that listening does not mean merely hearing what the automatic centres may manage to do, but that effective listening implies *pre*-listening all the time as to what *should be.* Explain to him that he must certainly listen to all he is doing — every note, but in the first place he must *want* every note aright. Say to him "do want all the time — every note." Be not taken up with the doing, but on the contrary "let Music tell you what to do" — let the piece, as it goes along, suggest to you what to do; then you may be sure that you are using your Imagination as well as your Reason. When the music seems to *tell* you what to do, then are you using your sub-conscious faculties as you should do eventually.

In short: during Practice do not try to "do," but try to *learn to see;* during Performance you may then be able to see Music — its Shape, Feeling and Time-spot, while you compel your fingers to give all this.

Granted, that training may possibly help to sensitise the actual ear-*machine* or apparatus — granted, also, that there may be a portion of our brain-matter more particularly engaged in aural work — the main point remains, and that is, that all ear-training in the first place signifies Mind-training: training ourselves to *observe* and *notice aural impressions*, training our mind to make use of the impressions received through our ear-apparatus. In short, Ear-training to be practical, must mean Mind-training, musically. Certainly, we should teach children Ear-attention from the very beginning, and from the simplest steps upwards.

But what is generally overlooked is, that every one professing to teach any form of musical performance must insist on such real Ear-training all day and every minute of every day when engaged in teaching — if it is to be real teaching at all.[1]

Definition of real practice. A passage must therefore never be played through, no, not even once through, except for the express purpose of really *knowing* that passage better; for the purpose of knowing it better not only physically but also mentally — knowing each bar better and the piece as a Whole better. Firstly, that we may know it better *as to its musical content* — both as to Shape and as to Feeling; and secondly, that

[1] Under the new faddism, I have heard of good teachers being turned out of schools on the ground that they, personally, have not acquired some particular stage of ear-discrimination, while no enquiry was made whether they were successful or not in making their pupils use their minds aurally. That the teacher possesses "absolute pitch" (relative pitch is another matter!) is no guarantee whatever that the possessor is in the least musical or observant aurally, or knows how to make others observant.

To insist on such a test is sheer folly. What should be insisted upon is, that the would-be teacher knows how to make *his pupils* use their own ears.

we may know it better *technically* — which means, that each playing through of it may help us to realise better *what to do physically*, and what to *avoid doing* physically at the keyboard.[1]

All this implies a constant process of analysis — of minute analysis as to what should be done and what *is* being done *musically* — and also, what should be done and is being done *technically*.

Constant process of analysis proved necessary.

Moreover, this again presupposes a high degree of concentration of mind on the part of the pupil, and that precisely *is* the requirement — full concentration of mind is needed. Now, it is the teacher's very first duty (and constant duty) to prompt the pupil in this direction.

True, such concentration may come almost "naturally" to the few possessors of that concatenation of various talents which the public loosely gathers up into the term *genius;* and if we do possess this so-called "genius," then

"Genius" implies natural concentration on one's work.

[1] Indeed, there is no practice worthy the name unless we are all the while really *studying;* studying (or *analysing*) with a most lavish, but carefully directed expenditure of thought and reasoning — and not one single note played without such expenditure. But a warning is also necessary here. From sheer wish to do right one may err. One may mistake *caution* for care. To be cautious — to be *afraid* of failing — will only chill one musically, and thus cause one to fail.

Practice implies study.

To be *afraid* of failure does not constitute a care for Music at all; on the contrary, it is again a form of selfishness, and as such must therefore cause failure. To succeed in art as in anything else we must be "unselfish," — so far as that is possible to us humans — we must throw self overboard, and really *caring for art*, we must wish to do well because art is so beautiful, so worthy, that any service we can bring to its shrine is as nothing. Thus we shall indeed take trouble, we shall be as keenly alert as lies within our power, not for the sake of our own aggrandisement, but for the sake of making the Beautiful attain to its highest possible perfection; and our "carefulness" will thus, so far from chilling us, stimulate us musically to ever increasingly effective efforts.

we may possibly succeed in giving such close attention without apparent effort, for the simple reason, that our bias towards Music is so extreme, and Music is such a keen delight to us, such a matter of life-and-death, that it is easy for us to be in this required state of keen engrossment, even, maybe, without much prompting from the teacher. But the teacher must ever be alert in such rare cases — for even a genius, we find, has frequent lapses of attention!

By learning concentration we can all approximate to the genius level. Now it also follows, that although our pupils may not all happen to be such "geniuses," we shall be able to bring them considerably nearer the genius-status if we can but manage to cultivate in them *this habit of close attention.* Anyway, to the extent that we do succeed in thus improving their powers of musical attention or concentration, to that extent they will certainly be *more musical* — and that is the point of the argument.

Not only concentration but imagination necessary. Please do not misunderstand me to maintain that such power of absolute attention is the attribute which, alone, constitutes genius.   Far from it!   To concentration we must add *vividness of imagination.* Here, indeed, we have the most salient feature of genius and of real talent—Imagination, the ability keenly to visualise, or auralise things apart from their actual physical happening outside of us.

The imaginative power must be trained. This more subtle faculty, imaginativeness — this power of *pre-hearing* — can also be cultivated in far greater measure than is generally suspected to be possible. Obviously this also is a task which the teacher must set himself to undertake, and must succeed in to some extent, if his pupils are to provide any real pleasure to their listeners.

Again, since it is clear that good practice implies a constant process of analysis, it must be still more clear that teaching implies the same process, persistently and unremittingly applied.

Now, in teaching, analysis implies (broadly speaking) analysis in four distinct ways:

The forms of analysis necessary in teaching.

Firstly, we must analyse WHAT THE PUPIL IS ACTUALLY DOING.

Secondly, we must analyse THE FAULTS THEREBY PERCEIVED.

Thirdly, we must analyse WHY THE PUPIL IS MAKING THOSE FAULTS; and

Lastly, we must analyse THE PUPIL'S ATTITUDE OF MIND, so that we may know how to treat him.

But before we can form any judgement at all, we ourselves must *know* the Music we wish to teach — *we* must have analysed that.

To be explicit on these four points:

Firstly: — We cannot become aware of all there is to be corrected, of all the faults made — and the good points made — unless we constantly analyse the impressions received from the pupil's performance; and this is what is implied by saying that the teacher must "really listen" all the while.[1]

Secondly: — The actual faults thus perceived (through such close listening) we must again analyse, so that we shall be able to diagnose them; for it is impossible to correct a fault *directly* or with certainty, unless it has been in the first place allocated either as a musical fault or as a muscular fault, or as one of laxity of attention, etc.

[1] Not listening, but merely hearing a performance, is just as useless in teaching as it is when examining, or learning, or practising. As I have already said, it is not enough merely to "hear," we must really listen, and plainly that means that we must all the while (to the best of our capacity) ANALYSE all we hear.

Thirdly: — We must analyse the particular pupil's *mental attitude* in making the fault, so that the fault-making may be corrected at its very root. For again, the fault may have arisen, for instance, either from inattention at the moment or inattention during practice; or its cause may be traced to bad habits muscularly, etc. ,

And here, especially, do not let us forget always to insist that all corrections, whatever their nature, must always be made strictly subservient to the *musical* effects required at the moment; else we shall only provoke self-consciousness in place of the desired correction. For instance, a muscular fault must never be corrected *as such*, but its musical bearing must always be kept before the pupil in each and every case.

Finally: — We must all the time closely analyse the pupil's *general mental attitude*, so that we may be able to judge how best to appeal to him (or impress him) so that our advice may be received sufficiently seriously as to lead to its being followed.

The use of example. While I thus insist that both teacher and pupil must constantly apply the analytical faculty, while I insist that reasons and causes must constantly be made clear to the pupil (musically and technically) nevertheless I do *not* maintain that actual Example, in the form of playing, is to be contemned. On the contrary, Example is most helpful *when given in conjunction with explanation,* especially with those who have the imitative gift strongly marked, or who can really feel Music keenly. Often, also, as a last resort, it has excellent effect.

The mistake is to rely *entirely* upon Example. This can lead only to subsequent disappointment, and with many pupils even to disaster, for the tendency, here again, is to

turn the pupil into an automatic machine, totally wanting
in initiative and in the where-with-all to acquire self-reliance.

Here we see the reason why the public artist is, as a rule, The artist as
so futile as a teacher — futile for the ordinary student, since teacher.
only the extremely gifted can learn anything whatever from
him. Such artist, as a rule, has usually not the remotest
notion *how* or *why* he does anything. Nor does he wish to
know; and he therefore has to rely in teaching solely and
entirely on this precarious device of exemplification.
If he ever did reason while learning, long ago has he forgotten
the process of learning. In fact, nothing is more antipathetic
to such artist, usually, than to be asked to reason upon
anything. . . . Long habit has indeed made it seem to him
that his own doings have "come naturally" to him and
have *not* been learnt, and must *not* be taught — in the way
one has to learn everything else in life. In fact, that it is a
sort of sacrilege, ever to want to know or to investigate the
being of Art, and that all that anyone should ever venture
to do, is to listen reverently and without question to his —
the artist's — supposed, God-given messages![1]

For the ordinary student to derive any profit from any
such exhibition of what may possibly happen to be quite
correct "doing," however, it is evident that it is he *himself*,
who will have to do all the reasoning and analysing unless
the processes are explained to him by some other teacher.

[1] One can in fact divide minds into two distinct types, the *informative* The informa-
and the *non-informative*, in the sense of either wanting-to-know or *not* tive and non-
wanting-to-know. I fear the artist is too often of the last-named type; informative
he likes to feel and enjoy, but he loathes the troublesome process of learn- types of
ing to understand the working of his own machinery. His gorge usually mind.
rises when there is any question of building-up or analysing anything in
his art . . . . . hence also the few BEETHOVENS, BACHS, and truly great
artists — and teachers! It is indeed a surprise and a delight to find
occasional exceptions to this rule.

True, the student, if gifted with extreme musical sensitiveness, may succeed in a measure in giving a photograph of what he has heard, but even then it will probably be but a pale or distorted version.

Such a great artist as *Liszt*, for instance, undoubtedly did have an overwhelming influence, musically, on all who came into contact with him. Nevertheless, he was *not* a real "teacher" at all, in the strict sense in which the term is here used — although he was truly a great SEER. Indeed, I doubt very much whether Liszt himself ever gave a single, real "lesson" in his life. What he did often do, with his overwhelming enthusiasm and wonderful personality, was to stimulate an incipient, latent, and perhaps lukewarm enthusiasm into a blazing flame.

A teacher must be artistic.

Nevertheless, while the artist is thus as a rule the most feeble of teachers, no teacher on the other hand is worthy the name unless he, himself, is also more or less an artist — and a finely perceptive one, too! To be a really good teacher, you must therefore possess, or at least you must have possessed a technique sufficiently ample to enable you to give due expression to the artistic feeling which you must have succeeded in cultivating in yourself.   So that, besides *really* teaching (i.e., explaining and showing), you may also be able to stir artistic fire and enthusiasm in others by actual example, when necessary.   Only then can you help your pupils in every way.

Why example, unaided, will not suffice.

As to the appeal solely to the imitative faculty, it is clear enough why this so often leads the pupil astray — often into sheer musical perversion; for indeed, a high degree of nice judgement is needed to perceive *what* it is that renders a musical performance good, or the reverse — to perceive what is essential and what is unessential. How can such nicety of judgement be expected from a mere School-student, seeing that it is this very thing you have to teach him? Indeed, he would require no teacher, did he already possess such power of judgement and of analysis.

Not possessing such highly cultivated power of observation or judgement, the student is almost bound to be captivated by some of the more prominent means of expression which you happen to employ in exemplifying to him, or possibly by some details of expression merely differing from those he has used. It is these which he will try to reproduce — with the best of intentions no doubt — but with the consequence that the picture will be quite out of focus, out of drawing, a picture probably much worse than it was before he tried to imitate that example which you gave him — remember, an example given *without explanation*, without the purpose and reason explained to him in so many words.[1]

Let us now consider what happens if we merely play through a passage to a pupil *without explanation*. I will play the opening bars of Schumann's "Warum" with the inflections of time and tone more or less correctly given, thus: Example v. explanation.

EXAMPLE 1.[2]

Rubato: riten. accel. - - - rit.→tempo   rit. accel. etc.

---

[1] We must never forget the fact that the most difficult problem for the pupil is to keep the picture in mind *as a whole* — as a continuous progression — and not to allow the *necessary* attention to each detail, as it comes along, to distract him from a persistent purpose to keep Shape and Outline perfectly clear.

[2] These time-inflections must be applied very subtly — not in a way so coarse as to call attention to themselves.

Without explanation given to him, the pupil will try to imitate the "means" — the expression-effects — he thinks he has heard me employ, and the result will probably be a frightful parody, with blind and futile changes of time and tone, such as the amateur who wishes to appear "musical" loves to make, something like this:

EXAMPLE 2.

But I shall obtain quite another result from the pupil, if I take the precaution thoroughly to *explain* the passage to him, either before playing it, or afterwards. For instance, I must first make the pupil *scan* the phrase correctly, so that he may understand its rhythmical structure — where its culminating point is, rhythmically, where "it goes to." Again, I must show him, that in music such as this, unless I bend or inflect the *time* as well as the tone (unless I give proper RUBATO to it) only squareness will result; and I must even point out exactly *how* the time is to be curved — *where* I must waste time to give emphasis, and *where* I must hasten the time so as to swing the rhythm back to the point where the phrase reaches its little climax, and in the meantime, and beyond all this, I must endeavour to convey to him its *emotional import*, either by gesture or word. In this way, and in this way only, the pupil will be made to understand *why* he must use the particular expression-means I used in exemplifying, and he will then also be able to use such musical sense as he has to guide him to the required *proper proportions.*

The result will now be a *real* performance, one prompted by his own mind in the right way. Moreover, it will display his own individuality, and it will be satisfactory, just because one can perceive in hearing it, that it is guided by the performer's *own* intelligence.

Furthermore, the pupil will also have made a step forward in his general knowledge of playing — a permanent step forward. Or, at all events, he will have had the opportunity of making it, provided his memory is good enough — for he will have had a lesson in *learning to analyse* and to apply means to an end.

There remains to be referred to, one more *general* characteristic which we, teachers, must cultivate in ourselves, and it is an important one. I have insisted that we should do our best to educate ourselves into being deft players as well as analytical teachers, but our efforts will after all be foredoomed to failure, if we expect our pupils *in cold blood* to give such truly exhausting attention as I have proved to be imperatively necessary. Such attention cannot be given in response to mere cold reasoning by itself, however logical; there must be a stronger motive force than this; there must be an *emotional* driving force to enable us to give this required attention — we must act under the stress of Feeling or Emotion; in short we must be prompted by ENTHUSIASM. *[side note: Necessity of enthusiasm.]*

Plainly, the teacher cannot hope in the least to stimulate his pupils to do real, honest work, unless he, the teacher himself, shows that the work *matters to him,* in fact, that it is a matter of life-and-death to him, whether his pupil does succeed or not, and whether the piece discussed is rendered adequately or not.

Imagination, hard work, yes, they are the fuel, but Enthusiasm is the spark which makes the whole leap into flame.

But some will object, that this is useless talk, that enthusiasm is purely a personal characteristic, and that we are either *made* that way, or are not. . . .   Well, one must concede that there is some truth in this.   But, on the other hand, if we try to recognise the fact that we shall be but miserably ineffective teachers unless we do summon up some real interest in our work, it will at least make us try better than before.

Again, the very fact of our thus trying to attend better and more minutely will, in its turn, inevitably lead to our finding it more and more easy to do so, since the exercise of a faculty always increases its efficacy; and in the end we may realise that it *really is worth while* trying to help and improve others. . . .   And our enthusiasm in our work will assuredly grow, when we see better and better fruits accrue from our better efforts.

The attempt to do work without giving one's whole mind to it, is indeed a very Hell upon earth, and *vice versa*, there is no finer Heaven, there is nothing more stimulating, than just this feeling, that our whole life is in our work, and that evidently *we are of use to our fellows.*

Bad and good teaching. I have dwelt upon the urgent necessity of the teacher using his brains all the time; let us next consider *how* he must use them.   Just as important as actually giving our mind to our work, is it, that we apply ourselves in the right way.   It is not enough to be thoroughly anxious to help our pupil; our hard trying will after all end but in sore disappointment unless we know *what* help to give and *how* to give it.

Here we are face to face with one of the most subtle and yet most radical of the distinctions between good teaching and bad — one of the most radical distinctions between the work of the inexperienced or foolish teacher, young or old, and that of a real teacher, rich in correctly assimilated experience. As I have said before: the bad teacher simply tries to make the pupil *do things* — "things," points, effects which the teacher feels are necessary; whereas the good teacher tries to make the pupil see and *think things*, so that, seeing their purpose, he can apply them by his own choice.   To be more explicit, simply to make the pupil Cramming v. carry out the details of expression and interpretation which realteaching. seem desirable to you at the moment, only serves to convert your pupil into an automaton, an automaton responsive to *your* thoughts instead of his *own* — a Trilby to your Svengalism. This is in fact sheer, miserable "cramming." Such cramming can have no abiding influence whatever on the pupil, for you are not in the least *educating* him — not in the least training his mind. It is doubtful, indeed, whether you will obtain from him, in that way, even one satisfactory performance.   No, the only way to establish any abiding improvement in your pupil, and also the only way to obtain, immediately, a vivid performance, is patiently and ceaselessly to insist on the pupil himself always using his own ears (upon the actual sounds, and upon the sounds that *should* be), his own judgement, his own reason and his own feeling; and this, not merely "in a general sort of way," but for every note, intimately, so that the musical picture, as a *whole*, may be successful.

This does not imply less attention on your part as teacher;

on the contrary, it implies far greater attention; for you
have to be as it were a vigilant policeman, constantly on
the alert, seeing to it that your pupil *keeps his mind on his
work* all the time, and does play every note as it should be
played.   Instead of acting as a bad orchestral conductor, you must act like a good conductor at rehearsal,
you must explain to your pupil the most intimate details
of structure and of feeling, so that he may musically be
able to see and feel rightly, and may therefore play rightly
because of thus seeing and feeling.[1]

In short, instead of the pupil being made merely to carry
into effect the means of expression dictated by you, he must
be made to use *his own musical imagination* and judgement
all the time, and also, what is equally important, his physical
judgement in connection with the instrument he is using —
as Pianist he must be using his sense of key-resistance, etc.,
all the time.

You must insist on his doing this all the time he is in your
presence, and you must try to induce him to do so all the
time you are absent.

To render a pupil " musical." A pupil generally plays badly, just because neither of
these things are done — unless, of course, he has not mastered
the right ways of Technique itself, in which case he will
play badly for the simple reason *that he is unable to express
what he does feel and think.*   But indeed you will often
find, that the moment you really succeed in making a pupil

Bad and good conducting. [1] The difference between a good and bad orchestral conductor depends
on the same laws: the bad conductor treats his men like machines —
tries to play on them, whereas the really great conductor tries to make
his men into intelligent artists, each one of them, tries to make them see
the music, and insists on their using their own musical feeling — in response to his, it is true, but not in mechanical obedience to his orders, or
bandmasterly directions.

attend musically and physically, that moment all his playing becomes infinitely more musical.[1] Much that seemed hopelessly wrong from the very foundations upwards, at once becomes better, and often to a quite surprising extent; and a pupil who perhaps seemed "hopelessly unmusical" gradually seems to become endowed with quite musical instincts!

Before going any further, I must try to make this difference still clearer — the difference between Teaching and Cramming. I recur again and again to this point, and urge upon my Teacher-students that we must do real teaching and not mere illusive "cramming," and yet I find that the temptation to act merely the SVENGALI tends to master us, unless we constantly resist it. Indeed even the best of us are often enough on the verge of falling into this trap, ever ready for us. But remember, the moment we give way, that moment we cease to be real teachers or educationists. *Teaching v. cramming again.*

It is difficult to resist this temptation, and always carefully to draw the line between merely *conducting* a performance of our own through our pupil's fingers and correctly teaching him by prompting him to play by his own initiative, helped by our constant, careful analysis of Shape and Feeling, and by example when desirable.

The temptation is of course all the greater, when dealing with exceedingly un-alert pupils, so-called "un-musical" ones. This teaching-principle, however, applies everywhere. Always try to avoid making the pupils "do," always try to make them *think*. Again, in thus honestly trying to help your pupils in better fashion, and really trying to make them use their own brains, you are after all only *scolding and finding fault*, and are not really teaching, *Make sure of your diagnosis.*

[1] By "physically" is here meant the use of one's outer ear, and one's muscular sense — with regard to key-resistance, etc.

unless — and that is the crux of the thing — unless you properly diagnose and make clear the true *cause* of each fault.[1]

And here we dare not be careless. It behoves us not to accept too hurriedly the first explanation that offers, but always to make sure that we have seen the true cause, the ultimate cause of the pupil's going astray, for while there may be many things that *seem* to be the cause, we may yet fail to correct the pupil owing to our wrong diagnosis.

But all such generalities are not really helpful, since the unanalytical person cannot apply them.

Concrete cases. Let us therefore take a concrete example. Say, a pupil plays a passage unrhythmically, such a very ordinary fault as the following one for instance, in Chopin's Polonaise in A:

EXAMPLE 3.

— the left hand is here often played as a quintuplet instead of in the proper Polonaise-rhythm. It was thus misplayed only the other day by a pupil, and as a number of listeners

---

[1] Let me reiterate it, the radical difference between real teaching and useless cramming is that in cramming you make the pupil parrot your own thoughts more or less unintelligently, whereas, in really teaching, you not only point out to the pupil *where* he is wrong and what the right *effects* should be, but always point out also the cause, *the why and wherefore* of all faults, and hence the means of their immediate correction; and you thus stimulate the pupil to use his own judgement and feeling all the time — musically and technically.

were in the room (some of them teachers of some experience)
I thought I would ask these to explain the fault. Here
are some of the answers:

> "Sounds sloppy" — "must be played with more spirit,"
> — which was true enough, but was no explanation
> of the fault, — any more than were the following
> ones:
>
> "Not enough accent in the right hand!"
> "Not enough accent in the left hand!"
> "Tone too much the same in both hands!" (True
> enough, subsidiarily.)
> "Tone too heavy in left hand!" (Also true.)
> "It is clumsy — holds herself too stiffly."
> "Plays with too much arm-weight."   (They thought
> that would please me!)   But the pupil continued to
> play her quintuplet in the left hand.   Then they got
> warmer:
>
> "Does not play rhythmically."
> "Left hand is not in time."
> "Does not hold the first quaver long enough" (perfectly
> true, of course).
> "Plays the two semiquavers *too soon*."

Nevertheless, *none* of these answers (not even the later
ones) formed any true correction or analysis of the *cause*
of the fault. None went to the root of the matter. True,
the *result* of the fault was plain enough all the time — its
ill-effect, and in the end the unmusical result was also correctly enough located. But the pupil was not told *how the
fault had arisen*, nor *how* to correct it. . . . Hence, none
of these tentative "corrections" formed any real teaching
of the pupil.

How to correct inaccuracy of time-details. The only possible direction to give to her, the only possible *real teaching* of this pupil, here, was simply to point out, that she *had failed to attend to time at that particular spot*, and had therefore omitted to *notice* where (in Time) the first of those two semiquavers *should occur:*

EXAMPLE 4.

It sufficed to point out to her this lapse of Time-attention, and of course the correction was instantaneously accomplished. It was now a true correction, it will be noticed, because the pupil herself was made to *think* rightly, was made to use her own judgement in the matter — for she was shown where her own Time-attention had been slack and was shown the consequences of such slackness. Therefore, it was true teaching; for she had been shown not only *how* to correct this particular fault, but, if she tried to profit by this lesson, she had the opportunity of *improving herself abidingly*, she had learnt something that might last her lifetime.

Playing out of time means lack of attention. Believe me, no one ever plays "out of time" if he really *attends* to Time. The fault is that pupils *do not attend*, nay, even find it impossible to attend — but only because they have not learnt to do so. It is precisely such attention which you have to teach them, every pupil you have, and all the time.[1]

Uselessness of the metronome, as a time-teacher. [1] You see, therefore, how useless it is to hope to teach your pupils a sense of Time and Rhythm by merely beating time to their performances, or making them listen to *your* exhibition of a Time-sense. True, the force of example may have some little effect, and your pupils *may*

To take other and opposite instances, of technical short-comings:

A comparatively musical pupil, who is obviously trying hard to play a *cantabile* passage most soulfully and sympathetically, fails sadly, however, owing to bad touch-habits. Here it is of no use telling her to "sing the passage better," or to "play it more sympathetically." The only way to help her is to explain to her *how* to produce the singing effect easily and therefore successfully, i. e., by arm-lapse, flat finger, and careful attention to the necessary *crescendo* of speed during key-descent, and accurate "aiming" of the key-motion, etc. Faults arising from bad touch habits.

Or, in a related case, a pupil may play her *passages* "stickily" or unevenly; here again, it is useless merely to call attention to these defects — probably she notices them (to her sorrow) as much as you do. The only true correction

play tolerably in time while you are "pumping" away, or counting or shouting; but the moment they are left alone — as they have to be for most of their playing-time — they play just as badly as before, since you have not told them *how* to help themselves.   The only way to teach them is unremittingly to insist on their attending to their own sense of Time-throb or sense of Rhythm while you have the chance.   Do not allow their rhythmical attention to flag for a moment while they are with you.   Moreover, you, yourself, will have to be alert all the time, else your own Imitative-sense will cause you unconsciously to follow their lax pulse-feeling, and you, yourself, being misled, will fail to notice their aberrations from Time-continuity.   You must be alert all the while so that your own Time-sense may remain unshaken, and so that you may compare your pupils' doings (in this respect) with what you feel is imperative.

Hence, also, you realise the folly of imagining that a Metronome can serve as a Time-teacher.   You see, the pupil has to learn to play to a pulse-throb of his own making all the while; it is therefore of very little use indeed learning to pay obedience to an outside, machine-made Pulse-throb.   And in any case, a Metronome is apt to kill the finer Time-sense implied by Rubato.   But more about this anon.

is to show her the *cause* of her defects — probably a forearm held stiffly, rotarily, and the rotary exertions not adjusted accurately to each finger, or maybe, complete ignorance as to the evil effects of "key-bedding." Or, it may even be a case of one actually mistaught technically, a victim for instance of the doctrine of "holding the knuckles in" — the doctrine which has done such an inconceivable amount of mischief at so many of our schools for girls, and music schools here and elsewhere. In such case, it is of no use saying *"you must hold the knuckles up"* — that would only do harm. You must show and make clear, that if the finger is properly exerted and the arm is not forced down, the knuckles will then automatically assume their natural level position; and you must demonstrate that it is just as impossible to use one's fingers freely and easily at the Piano under such absurdly unnatural and helpless conditions, as it would be to take a walk with one's legs doubled up at the knee — in the crouching position assumed for a certain kind of comic race.

Correction of incorrect tempi. As two final instances: when a slow movement is played *too slowly*, do not say "play quicker"; instead, try to make the pupil *think* the music in *longer phrases.* Again, if a quick movement is played *too fast*, you will only hamper yourself, or your pupil, by telling him to "try to make the piece go slower"; instead, here draw attention to the *in-between beats*, or sub-divisions of these beats, and the result is immediately attained and with certainty.

The causes of faults must always be made clear. No, teaching does not consist in merely pointing out the existence of faults — not now-a-days — but in our always making clear the *cause* of each fault, and the direct means of its correction.[1]

---

[1] In other words: it is not enough to notice the *nature* of each fault and to point this out to the pupil, you must correctly diagnose the *cause* of each fault and explain that to the pupil.

You have to teach people to attend, to analyse, to *notice* on their own account — to notice and observe Time, and also everything else, Tone and Duration, *how* they should be, and also, *how they really appear;* and you also have to teach people *how* to obtain the required tonal effects from their instrument.

To teach people *how to attend* and *how to do,* — how to *feel* and *perceive,* that alone is real teaching, and it is a proud thing to be engaged upon. It is never "hack-work" — if you insist thus on really teaching people how to think, and do not try to make them use their fingers in response merely to *your* musical wishes. Only by bearing these things in mind can you avoid being a "crammer," and can you attain to being a true *educationist.*

True educa-tion.

SECTION II

THE NATURE OF MUSICAL ATTENTION AND OF MUSICAL SHAPE

WE have now realised how keenly close attention must be striven for by the pupil; this brings us to a consideration of the next practical question, *how* such attention is to be brought about immediately and inevitably.

Attention through key-resistance and time. The answer is the one I have already so often insisted upon — the only possible way of attending to Music during Performance is through that duplex form of attention, attention through *key-resistance*, and attention through *time*.

Whatever the passage, whether of the slowest *cantabile*, or the lightest and swiftest *agility*, we can only attend to it by unremittingly giving our minds, in the first place, to the requirements of the instrument itself, that is, to the *constantly varying resistance of the key* itself during its descent, corresponding to the various tones required.

And again, in the second place, it is only possible definitely to guide the forces we are thus prompted to expend, by definitely intending and accurately fulfilling a "Time-spot" for each note. In short, to enable us to attend to musical feeling we must (at the Piano) attend to the Key, through its every motion being exactly chosen and timed.[1]

---

[1] Is not this a strange paradox, that to enable us to play *musically* we must give close attention *mechanically* — through the key-lever; and in the same way, the fiddler must attend through his bow-pressure. Or, to be more accurate, in playing the Piano or Violin we must attend to our tones through the controlled (accurately adjusted) relaxation of our

Here then, we have *two* most definite and tangible facts upon which to keep the student's and artist's mind; and the inevitable corrollary of his thus attending *to key-motion* through *time*, is that he will also be compelled to give the closest and most intimate attention to Music itself — to musical Feeling and Shape. Concerning this question of Time-spot, I have very much more to say today, but concerning that of Key-resistance, I have so fully shown the way in my "Relaxation Studies" and elsewhere, that I need not enter further into this matter now, except perhaps to point out, that these same "Relaxation Studies" are indeed, many of them, merely teaching-devices for this very purpose — to teach the student how to attend to the key.[1]

Now as to the question of "Time-spot": if a violinist or singer does not give his mind to his work, his instrument warns him instantly and unmistakably, for his intonation becomes faulty, and that is a result which, usually, annoys him too much to be ignored. **Meaning of "Time-spot."**

Now at the Piano, inattention, it is true, may cause us to play actual wrong notes; but besides such mere "wrong notes," a far worse thing happens, for the very moment we allow ourselves to become inattentive as to the precise Time-spot of every note, that moment we do indeed play

arm-weight, and in singing through the controlled relaxation of our ribs. (*See* the late John H. Kennedy's "Common Sense and Singing" — real common sense on the subject.)

[1] The most important of these Studies (bearing on this particular matter) are the "Resting" and "Aiming exercises," "Throw-off," and "Agility" tests; and, most important of all perhaps, the "Rotation" exercises. In fact, it is impossible to play at all, unless the technical ground covered by such "tests" has been mastered to some extent. The extent of such mastery may indeed be said to form the limit of our technical attainments; which signifies, the *elimination* of all unnecessary exertions, and the accurate *timing* and choice of the required ones.

"out of tune" in a sense — that is, out of tune *as regards
time*. And this is far less a mere figure of speech than it
would appear to be at first sight, since both are vibrational
experiences.[1]

As I have before insisted upon, during performance it is
really impossible *definitely* to guide any note, unless we do
thus think of its Time-spot: the precise place in Time where
the sound is musically due to begin, and where the key's
motion is therefore due to *finish* its act of tone-production.
The most striking and most definite thing about a note is
the fact of its transition from *non*-existence to existence —
the moment of transition from Silence to Sound; for this
is an absolutely definite point of demarcation at the Piano,
as definite as the surface (or beginning) of a piece of wood
or stone.[2]

The act of thought or attention itself implies a rhythmical act.

We cannot, therefore, definitely think a note in playing
unless we thus *think* the time-place of its *beginning* — the
beginning of the sound.   Moreover, we must try to
realise, that this law has a far deeper significance even than
this.   The fact is, we cannot experience any act of consciousness, we cannot direct our minds and think about

Similarity between playing out of time and playing out of tune.

[1] We all know that a musical sound is the effect produced upon our
mind by the regular recurrence of impulses on our ear. What we call
"Time" in Music is, however, quite a similar experience; the recurrence
of pulse-throbs are similar to vibration-throbs, but in the first case the
recurrences are enormously slower. Hence it is useful and suggestive to
remember that "playing out of time" is an evil effect belonging to the
same genus as *playing out of tune*; it is just as unclean, sordid and disheartening, just as unnatural, unbeautiful, and un-godly!

[2] In other words, the only way definitely to guide into existence any
note at the Piano. is clearly to determine the moment when this transition
from Silence to Sound is musically due, and to see to it that we so carefully
guide the Piano key-lever that it will *finish* its work of tone-production
at that precise moment — the moment which we have in our mind musically.

or realise anything definitely, without just such an act of *timing* — a timing of our consciousness.   The act of bringing or directing our thought or attention upon anything is therefore a *rhythmical process;* Thought and Rhythm are inseparable.   Again, we see the reason why in the absence of Rhythm there can only be Nothingness — emptiness, non-being![1]

We must insist, therefore, on the pupil clearly realising " Grip " in that he can only obtain "grip" of what he is doing by performance. means of close attention to this fact, *that he must finish* each act of tone-production at the very moment his Time-sense impels him to *wish* each note to *begin.*   Having thus something definite to take hold of mentally, this will enable him to think also of the colour he wishes to give each note, its place in the phrase, its place as part of a whole.

Now here arises the question, how shall we make a pupil As to time-understand Time and Rhythm, and why do so few seem to training. feel it at all?   The fault usually arises either from the entire want of, or fault in, early training in this respect.

The fact is, no child should ever be allowed to sound a note at the Piano until his Time-sense has been thoroughly aroused.   It is the very first thing, and the most supremely important thing to teach.

Before teaching the note-signs, or even the note-*sounds,* we must teach attention to Pulse.   We must make the

---

[1] The term "Rhythm" is of course in this work used in its proper and As to the all-embracing sense, its narrowest and its widest application, and including interpreta-bar-rhythm, figure-rhythm, phrase-rhythm — the minute rhythm implied tion of the in the ever-changing sub-divisions of the bar pulses, as well as the huge term rhythmical swing of a whole phrase played *as one single pulse* in Rubato, " rhythm." and the still greater Pulse of a real master-piece when this swings on to its climax with unbroken continuity of purpose — a Whole, which, built up of multifarious ideas and logical successions, is yet welded together as we find it only in the works of the really great composers.

beginner realise that Pulse (the recurrence of *time-distances*) is a material fact, quite easy to realise if only we attend to it; and he should have considerable facility in the appreciation of Pulse and its subdivision before he is allowed to touch the keyboard at all. And when he does so, we must from the first insist on his realising that every note he plays must be accurately fitted into the particular Pulse-scheme chosen by him *as the canvas* upon which to paint his musical picture — and this, however simple the picture may be.[1]

Correct idea of time and shape in music. This brings us to a very important matter: the correct outlook as to what is meant by Time in Music — important indeed, for if this outlook is incorrect, our whole outlook on Music will necessarily be based on a foundation of sand.

Now we shall find that although the arts of Music and Painting seem so very different, yet we have here a strong parallelism in the basis of both, inasmuch as both depend upon Progression or Movement.

Progression and movement analogous in music and painting. In painting or drawing the *movement is upon the canvas*, and this in a double sense; for there is, first, an actual *movement* of the painter's brush or pencil in the act of making the picture; and secondly, an actual *movement* again, in viewing the picture — an actual movement *of our eyeballs* in following its lines, or at least a suggestion of such movement.

The origin of our sense of pulse. [1] That is, the pupil's mind must be brought to notice the phenomenon of Pulse or Beat. This is best done by calling attention to the swing of his stride in walking or running; and remember, he had to learn to feel pulse in a measure before he could encompass either of those accomplishments! Indeed, I opine, that in our gait, we have the *origin* of our feeling of pulse in music. We *imagine* the swing of a walking or running stride; we set one going for every piece we play, and imagining its continuance it thus guides us. How vivid do the Beethoven themes become if we hum them in our rambles through the woods — conceived as so many of these themes doubtless were under a similar impression of fresh air and the accompaniment of a healthy walking stride.

In Music the distinction is, that the movement is upon a *time-surface,* as it were — instead of upon a canvas.

Here then, we have two very close analogies in Music and Painting, unexpected though they may be: (I) This sense of Progression, or Movement, and (II) this necessity of some *medium* upon which to fix our progressions.

In Music we choose some particular sequence of beats or pulses, and upon this particular form of *extension in space,* or Time-spacings, upon this thoroughly tangible *time-canvas* of Pulse we lay out the *progression* of our musical picture, whether as composers or players — just as the painter must lay out his work on *his* canvas.

It may strike you at first that all this is "a very waste of words" but I assure you we are here face to face with one of the fundamental laws of our art, and the teaching of it. Yes, even the uncultured members of an audience can quite well *feel* the effect of rhythm, or its absence. When the Rhythm is strong, they are impressed by the fact that the piece is alive, but when the Rhythm is lax, or Time-continuity is broken up, they feel that it is "as dead as a door nail"; and this, although quite unaware of the cause of their comfort or discomfort. Indeed, so strong is this rhythmical need of the public, that when rhythmical grip is lacking in a performer no other attractions offered by him can save the piece.[1]

Here we have indeed one of those fundamental facts which we must drive home to every pupil, even beginners. It is

---

[1] We also find that our musical ideas of "Time" and "Progression" are closely correlated; since to enable us to determine the precise "time-spot" of any note, we must think of music itself — in its aspect of progression or movement. And, *vica versa*, attention to musical Progression will also, in its turn, compel our attention to the details of Time and Pulse.

of no use trying to *think* Music unless you think of *progression*, that is, Movement *towards* something or other.

In fact, this forms the best definition of all Form or Shape or Structure in Music, be it phrase, section, sentence or a complete piece. This idea of Movement is the vitalising spark which turns mere notes into living music, this sense of Purpose — this sense of *progressing somewhere*.[1]

The progressional view of music v. the old segmental view. It is astounding that until lately none of the Theory-teachers seem to have put this fact into words; although, of course, no real musician has ever *felt* music apart from an *unconscious* appreciation of this fact.[2]

Instead of Progression — continuous, purposeful Movement — they have tried to explain Music as consisting of *chunks* or solid segments of accented bars and of unaccented bars, thus giving the mis-impression to the learner, that Music consists of dead, disconnected bits of sound-stone or brick, instead of a living mass, a continuous swing and swirl of Growth.[3]

This idea of *motion* in Music, continuous Movement, we must make clear to anyone and everyone, even to a child at his very first lesson in Music.

Having applied this teaching principle for the last twenty years or so, and knowing its electrifying effect on the student,

[1] A phrase, for instance, may therefore in performance be defined as: a growth, or progression of notes towards a cadence, shown by means of Tone and Rubato inflections.

[2] My old pupil, John B. McEwen, has of course adopted this teaching of mine in his admirable "Phrasing"; and now, on going to press with this MS (October, 1912) I receive a copy of a new work of his just issued, "The Thought in Music," a work full of original thought and research wherein he develops this idea still further and with a masterly hand.

[3] In the "Coda" of this work (Section IV) it will be seen why this progressional view of Music-structure is so vitalising to the student, artist, and teacher.

I tried to call attention to this necessity in the final chapter of my "First Principles," page 126; but most people seem to pass this passage by, without noting that it bears indeed on all they do every day as teachers. This is what I mean by "scanning" the music before trying to play it; the rhythmical shape or *progress* of even the simplest phrase must be understood, if we are to have any chance of playing it correctly, and if our performance is not to drivel into mere musical — or unmusical — babbling.[1]

[1] This doctrine of Progression or Movement, which I insist upon as the basis of all Shape in performance, is indeed a most important teaching principle — one might say perhaps *the* most important of all. The old way of teaching Form, Form-analysis, Structure, and Interpretation with its false ideas of dead, disconnected segments of music (blocks or chunks) was perfectly useless, musically, to the student. It not only failed to give him any real insight into what constitutes Music in the act of performance, but it failed to draw his attention to Movement as the basis of all Music, and it was therefore positively deadening from a performing point of view. The *progressional* teaching of Musical Structure is on the contrary at once vital, helpful, and interesting to every Music-student, whatever his status, and whatever his branch of study. In my own personal teaching and lectures, I had for many years enforced this principle of "towardness" as the basis of all Music-shape — the basis of all music-teaching, but the idea was not made public in *printed* form until the issue of my "Act of Touch" (page 42) in 1903, and my *"First Principles"* in 1905 — *see* page 126, where the practical application of this study is summarized. In the present lectures (written in 1909) it was of course developed and amplified still further.   It is a source of great gratification to me to find that it is now being generally accepted, at least by the more up-to-date Theory teachers of this country. For instance, in a recently issued work (1912) on "Phrasing and Form" I find the following — practically a quotation from a *synopsis* of this present lecture published in "The Music Student" of April, 1911, and of which Synopsis a reprint is given in the Appendix to this work: "The next matter to which attention "must be directed in order to arrive at any intelligent basis for our phrasing "is the fact that everything in music must be considered in the light of "progression, or movement towards some more or less clearly defined desti-

The difference between the old *segmental* view of structure, and the *progressional* view of musical structure.

When we teach a baby to say "Mamma" and "Papa" we do try at the earliest possible moment to make him realise that "Papa" and "Mamma" do mean something definite; in fact that these sounds stand for two very definite and important people! Nevertheless, in teaching the child to talk through the Piano, the inconceivable folly is committed of allowing him to babble — to make unmeaning noises; and this, often until he is an adult, without any attempt to make him realise that Music consists of words and phrases — connected sound-movements — like any other language![1]

Some examples of the progressional view of structure. As this idea of looking for Shape in the sense of progression — or "scanning" — may be unfamiliar to many of you, let me give you some examples of what I mean. Let us take the first half of "God Save the King," as one of the simplest of tunes. It consists as you know of three *bits*, each bit with its little climax, and the third "bit" forming a capping climax to the other two. That is, the first bar *progresses* to

"nation. This is true whether we have in our thoughts the gradual but "inevitable working up of some extended passage towards a strong emo-"tional climax, or of the no less essential 'trend' of some figure of a few "notes towards the point where it finds its own completion," etc. Further quotations occur on subsequent pages; and finally, it is gratifying to find in the preface of his work, that the author gracefully acknowledges the source of these teachings, and that he has presented them with delightful conciseness.

[1] The root of the trouble is that children are taught Music the wrong side up. The usual false beginning is to try to make them associate paper signs with keyboard-places, instead of beginning, as one should do, by trying to make them recognise actual sounds, actual Time, and Music-shapes, — matters which are mostly left to dawn upon them later on, as an afterthought! Mrs. Spencer Curwen, in her admirable "Child Pianist," started the crusade against this topsy-turvydom, and her views are more and more rapidly gaining ground, as we see by the various imitators who have adopted her ideas.

the second (at *a*), the third bar to the fourth (at *b*), and the
fifth bar to the sixth (at *c*), thus:

EXAMPLE 5.

We find a similar structure, and it is a very usual one,
(two short, or less accented progressions capped by a longer
or stronger one) in the opening of Schumann's first Novellette.   From the barring of this (totally incorrect as it
is) one would imagine, that the piece was meant to sound all
upside-down musically, thus:

EXAMPLE 6*a*.

Schumann's Novellette played with accentuation as barred in the
original.

But of course he did *not* mean this; therefore here, as so
often elsewhere, we must totally disregard the written bar-
lines (or written accentuation) and must be led by our own
musical sense; and we then find that this opening phrase
consists of *three progressions*, each moving towards its little
climax or crisis, and the three together moving or progressing

towards a more important climax — that of the complete
phrase. Thus:

Example 6*b*.

Schumann's Novellette, played with *correct* accentuation, requiring
the bar-places as denoted by the dotted lines at *b* (and not at *a* as in the
original).[1]

The incor-
rect notation
of bar-lines.

[1] Composers, in the past (and many in the present), do not seem to
have realised the simple fact, that the only possible real use of a bar-line
is to indicate to the performer *where* the pulse-swing should be.

To prevent monotony, a musical composer will often purposely alter
the straight course of the accentuation, and an unmusical or inexpert
composer still more frequently does so from the want of fine feeling, or
from ignorance; but both types seem equally to be obsessed with the idea
that if bar-lines are but written down in unbroken sequence (so as to *look*
symmetrical) this will ensure symmetry, or that this will throw dust in
the eyes of people, and make them believe the work to be symmetrically
perfect — like wallpaper! As a matter of fact, no musician does want
wall-paper patterns instead of music, nor does the placing of the bar-lines
where they are *not* wanted by the sense of the music, alter the accentuation
one jot. The only result such obsession, carelessness or ignorance can
have is to puzzle the performer, and to ensure that unmusical players
will perform the piece musically "upside-down." Even many of the
great Masters have sinned sorely in this matter of the true notation of
their works, Schumann and Brahms perhaps most of all; whereas Beethoven's notation is perhaps most free from this blemish. In the old poly-
phonic writing there was of course the difficulty, that bar-lines would have
been required separately for each part, certainly a chaos when four or

As one more example of this structure, let me quote from the slow movement of Beethoven's Sonata, Op. 2, No. 2, — thus:

EXAMPLE 7.

Or pictorially, it might be shown thus:

EXAMPLE 8.

All this shows us clearly how the idea of ʹphrase, or sentence, implies *progression* towards some more or less definite point; by this sense of progression, of his *being led somewhere*, the listener's attention is attracted, and is retained.[1]

more parts were written on two staves only; but why in such a case put bar-lines at all, where they can only be mis-leading?

As one more glaring instance of such wrong barring see Chopin's Prelude in C minor — the true bar-line occurs two pulses later than the written bar-line.   But such cases are innumerable.

[1] As to the word "phrase": it really does not signify whether we consider the musical *unit* to be a "motif," "idea," "section," "phrase," or "sentence."   All this is purely a matter of mere nomenclature, music-terminology — a point of exceedingly small importance artistically.   What does matter is that bar-lines should be recognised as denoting the general swing of the accentuation, and that Music-units (or the more complex "phrase" or "sentence" organisms) are always in themselves again *progressions* towards definite landmarks.

As to nomenclature of structural details.

We shall moreover find that this sense of *going somewhere* implies that there must be a *succession* of *harmonies* (actual or implied) either forming or leading up to some form of harmonic cadence; we *must* have this, if there is to be any definite idea of Shape in what we accept as Music.

Let us now try to transcribe "God Save the King" so that it shall suggest (as far as possible) *only one harmony;* hear how this impoverishes the tune, thus:

EXAMPLE 9.

Or better still, let us try to compose a theme solely on one harmony, and we shall find that because it *goes* nowhere harmonically, nothing seems to happen. (*See* Exp. 10a.)

EXAMPLE 10a.

Whereas, if we now alter the same theme slightly, so that it may take harmonies, you will see how much more clear and interesting it at once becomes:

EXAMPLE 10*b*.

You see now, that the term "harmonic progression" is really a most apt and suggestive term; for you see, that a mere succession of un-related or un-progressive sounds or chords is quite meaningless. To have any meaning, musically, we require a *progress* of chords, intelligently leading towards definite landmarks, the landmarks in key and rhythm which we call "cadences."[1]

---

[1] Incidentally, you should here note, that the very process itself of learning, or assimilating any knowledge, is of this very same nature — it is but a form of progression.

The process of memorising also depends upon progression.

Isolated facts mean nothing; *to memorise anything* the only possible process is to bring the something you wish to memorise into some form of *progression*, or sequence *of thought*. That is, you must *chain* the something you want to fix in your mind *to* something *already* stored there; you must make use of something you already know, so that it shall *suggest* (as a mental progression) the something fresh which you want to fix in your memory.

In a word, you must build-on to the knowledge you already do possess further *progressions* of "onwardness," mentally.

In the case of Musical-memory, each note, each chord you play, must

Deliberate indefiniteness in composition. True, in some few isolated instances, the composer has purposely written unclear, shapeless, jelly-like music, and not inadvertently, as only too often happens. Wagner, for

be made to *suggest* the next note or chord, etc. And unless you have made a *perfect chain* of such suggestion-connections, you do not remember and cannot remember any piece. In short, remembrance of a piece means that the suggestion-channels are all in good working order.

How to apply one's memory. *Vice versa,* successfully to make use of the memory-connections thus stored in your mind, you must during performance *allow* the thing present and realised at the moment to *suggest* (as an automatic or reflex action) the thing which is to follow on. That is, you must *allow* the memory of each succeeding portion of the text to be automatically revived by the rhythmic swing of the portion of the passage you *are* playing at the moment, its melodic and harmonic progression, its mood, and each note of it in succession.

In short, you must *allow* your memory-stream to flow in the channels or courses you have previously made for it, and the only way to prompt these memory-connections into action is by keeping your mind vividly present *on the actual thing you are doing at the moment;* and you cannot help your memory by trying to recall the thing ahead; since this will disconnect or destroy the sequential action of your mind.

Memory failure. The moment you begin to doubt your memory's capacity to "follow on," that moment you will hinder, if not completely stop its action. *If* you commit the fatal blunder of *trying to recall the next note,* this will at once paralyse the natural and safe action of the previously-made memory-channels; you will thus stop their flow, and your mind will seem to be a blank as to what comes next.   Here it is not a case of your memory being incomplete or unreliable, but simply that you are *preventing* its natural action. Either the mental successions of "onwardness" are there, or they are not. If they are complete they will act with certainty if you let them do so; whereas, if they are not properly fixed in your mind, then no attempt to recall the *next* note will help you one jot.

In other words, if these mental connections or chains have been properly linked-up, you can only stimulate them into action by bringing your attention vividly upon the point you *are* engaged upon at each moment during the performance of the piece — so that it may suggest what follows. Whereas you will inevitably paralyse this natural sequential action,

instance, has used this device in the Introduction to "Das Rheingold" so as to give the vague, impalpable effect of

if you try to wrench your mind on to something ahead, — something not yet actually due in performance.

On the other hand, if these progression-suggestions are not firmly fixed in your mind, you must take steps to strengthen them, on the lines above indicated.

Here it is well to realise, that musical memory is a complex phenome- **The various** non. We must take care to use *all* the available memory channels; and **kinds of** they can only be rendered available by the application of close analysis, **musical** consciously or unconsciously given. These components are on the one **memory.** side purely musical, but on the other side are technical, instrumental and muscular, or gymnastical.   Hence we must analyse and thus memorise the musical progressions of the piece, its rhythmical, melodic and harmonic progressions, and above all things the inflections of its moods or poetic curves.   But besides this strictly-speaking *musical* memorising of the piece we must also impress our eye-memory with the written page, and with the *lie* of the music on the keyboard — as keyboard progressions.

Added to all this, we must also apply our muscular-memory — we **The neces-** must fix in our mind the physical sensations of its note-successions upon **sity of mus-** the keyboard, and the technical methods of their execution. **cular memory**

And it is just here where all the trouble begins: on the one hand, it **and its** is impossible to give one's mind to the musical interpretation of a *quick* **dangers.** movement, unless we do know the notes of it so well that we need no longer question what they are. To succeed in this, however, for a quick movement, we must have repeated its note-successions often enough to impress them thoroughly upon our automatic-centres, so that our fingers may be able to find the road automatically. Now the imminent danger always is, that in trying to acquire this necessary part of the performance-memory, we may totally destroy all our musical control over the piece.   It is this same automatic necessity which so often leads players astray into the acquisition of purely automatic and mechanical methods of practice.

The only remedy and preventive is constantly to insist on *musical* **Silent** *attention;* and often to practice *without touching the keyboard at all.* With **practice.** our fingers upon the keyboard, it is only too easy to forget to direct them; hence the great value of silent practice, with every note-inflection

water. It is all on the chord of E flat, you remember the rising flowing figure:

EXAMPLE 11.

He wishes to convey the idea of a mass of water, the Rhine, not seen as a definite sheet of water, but seen from *within* the water, from inside the river; and he could not have chosen a happier way of making the musical suggestion than by the means used. It has no surface, no bottom, and after ten minutes of it or so, you feel yourself floating in the swirl of the river — with the Rhinemaidens — and

imagined, and its impossibility of allowing the attention to flag, even for a moment. And when actual keyboard-practice is imperative during the process of acquiring the necessary automaticity in respect to the keyboard successions of the notes, even in this case never to allow our musical purpose to waver, never to allow our automatic, or gymnastic faculty to gain the upper hand and to fulfil its sway without our constantly directing and controlling it musically by our *mind*-centres — our will-power, our musical imagination and judgement.

To prevent slithering. To ensure such control we must constantly re-analyse the *rhythmical* constituents, or rhythmical *landmarks* of every agility-piece, however old an acquaintance it may be. The moment we thus insist on compelling the automatic centres to *fit their work* to our rhythmical vision, that moment the piece no longer seems to "run away," but is instead perfectly guided by our musical conscience. Hence also in performance, we must always insist on realising the TIME-PLACE, for each note; and our gymnastic faculty thus becomes our obedient servant and not our master. See page 29 on "Time-spot," page 30 "The act of consciousness," and page 53 "Wrong bass notes," also page 122 "On the memorising of fingering." Also see *Additional Note:* "The cause of stammering unmusically," page 59.

cannot think of them as stage people, swinging about on iron cages![1]

This law of Progression in Music applies not only in the case of the phrase or the sentence but applies universally, as much to the smallest details of the music as to its largest swings of form.   As I have already pointed out in "First Principles" and elsewhere,[2] no one (not even a child-beginner) should be allowed to sound any succession of sounds, however simple, without being made clearly to understand that there must be *some* shape or progression even in such primitive attempts; thus:

EXAMPLE 12.

Not 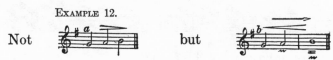 but

— therefore in fact suggesting harmonies; for instance:

EXAMPLE 13.

[1] Someone has asked, "What should we call this passage, there is no 'phrase' really in question, there being no harmonic progression?"   I should define the figure as an *idea-unit* which, purposely, is not allowed to become definite enough to form a "phrase."

Purposely, Wagner has left the Prelude ambiguous, sheer invertebrate musical protoplasm, without any higher organisation of definite shape; its swelling, musically jelly-like indefinite mass thus accomplishes its purpose dramatically and scenically.

[2] "First Principles of Pianoforte Playing," page 126, and in "The Child's First Steps."

You must next realise that it is from non-perception of this very point (non-preception of the fact of progression) that results all the rhythmical "sloppiness" so lamentably rampant; I refer to that unclear playing of passage-work, unclear execution of minute contrasts in the lengths of the notes, details seemingly so insignificant, yet upon the accuracy of which depends so much of our enjoyment of the music.[1]

How often indeed do we find the inexperienced (or bad) teacher's pupils playing triplets or quadruplets of notes all clipped together, thus:

EXAMPLE 14.

Do you see the cause of this fault?

It is clear enough, when you realise that you *cannot think music* (that is rhythm) unless you always definitely think of its Progression — we are constantly compelled to come back to this point!

To correct a fault of this nature, all you have to do then is to make the pupil realise that the triplet or quadruplet, etc., does *not* finish with the beginning of the sound of its last note, but, on the contrary, that the group lasts *up to the beginning* of the first note of the *next group* — the next pulse-throb. Thus:

EXAMPLE 15.

[1] In playing, the terms clearness and cleanliness refer to two distinct things; "clearness" refers to rhythmical accuracy, while "cleanliness" refers to the sounding of the right notes — without any "splitting" of them, etc.

20a.

(Incorrectly played.)

...not allow yourself to think of the two hands, as each ...ing something independently, but insist on thinking ... passage as *continuous*, rhythmically; think of it in ... of six semiquavers, each one leading *up to* the begin-... each next group, and the supposed "difficulty" at ...anishes forever. Thus:

20b.

(Correctly played.)

...rule of course also holds good when the passage is of ... notes in each hand, instead of octaves; also, when ...ernations between the hands occur after several notes ...been taken successively by each hand — when the ...ations between the hands occur after whole groups of

You must show him, that *time* in music always implies the *dividing* up of Space; and in this particular concrete case, that it means movement in equal divisions of time always *up to* the next following pulse-throb.

In short, you must always think of the beat ahead, must always lead up to it, *divide up towards it*, if the "inside" notes of passages are to be clear to the listener.

And this rule applies not only when you have the "inside" notes (or in-between notes) *evenly* distributed between the pulses, but also when you have more complex rhythmical figures providing the in-between sounds, such as:

EXAMPLE 16.

Moreover, it applies when you have figures ending with *unaccented notes;* and it applies still with equal force even when you have a whole phrase or sentence moving towards its rhythmical climax with a decrease of tone.[1]

Progression always towards climax of phrase in spite of decrescendo

Let me give you an example of both points:

In Chopin's first Prelude we have a figure with such unaccented ending:

EXAMPLE 17.

[1] We shall see later on, that *Rubato* must here come to our aid to make clear the onward striving of the phrase.

In the second subject from Beethoven's Sonata Op. 22, we have the second point illustrated, as well as the first.[1]

EXAMPLE 18.

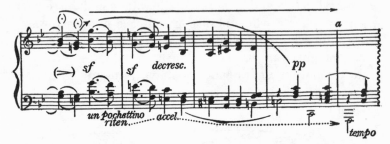

---

[1] At first sight this Beethoven excerpt, from Op. 22, almost looks like a case of misplaced bar-lines; but it is quite correctly barred, for the *sfs* are here true syncopations, which are felt to go against the true rhythmical pulse, and which last must persist in spite of these *sfs*. The bar-line (or true pulse) may be shown by making the notes *on* it slightly staccato, as I have suggested. The whole tune grows towards the chord of *F* at (*a*). This is made clear by employing a very slight *rubato* during the last four bars — very slight indeed, so slight as to be unnoticeable even to pedantically-inclined ears.

Again, in Beethoven's 32 Vari[ations] such figure with unaccented e[nd]tion:

EXAMPLE 19.

You see, in all these cases, the at its end, before reaching the unless we keep that next pulse a we *measure* the places for the e towards such pulse — we canno[t] Time, and our performance will musically.

Again, in passages divided (or such as octave-passages, etc., ho[w] these rhythmically, by clipping t hands.

The remedy is simple enough, the same nature. Simply insist the passage being thought of as succession in) rhythm; it must n[ot] of *two hands, each doing somethi[ng]* rhythmically disconnected.

For instance, the semiquaver Mendelssohn's Rondo, Op. 14, ar[e]

EXAMPL[E]

Do one d such group ning once

Th SING the a have alter note[s]

We must, however, bear in mind that such rhythmical Broken faults do often and quite easily arise in such alternating passages, passages from quite another cause, and that is from faulty technical errors. Key-treatment — faulty Touch-habits.

In fact, such passages are often thus *made* "difficult," simply by disobedience to "the Law of Resting," which I have so strongly insisted upon in my various works on Touch and Technique.[1]

Indeed, the law of continuously *resting* upon the keyboard during the extent of each phrase may never be disregarded with impunity, not even in the case of "divided" passages. The point to remember, therefore, is that in all such passages (passages divided between the hands) the keyboard *must never be quitted by one hand until the* next *hand has a finger on its own first note;* the passage is thus linked-up continuously in a chain of "Restings," alternately taken up by the successive hands, and without break during the course of each phrase.   For instance:

Not thus:

EXAMPLE 21a.

---

[1] Refer also to page 53 *re* "Wrong Bass-notes," etc.

But thus:

EXAMPLE 21b. (Prelude and Fugue, Mendelssohn.)

(The lecturer here showed how each hand in succession carries on the continuity of contact with the keyboard — the hands rising off the keyboard, but each one remaining in contact with it until the next has found its note.)

The following two excerpts are also suggestive:

(From Concert-piece in A minor, Tobias Matthay.[1])

EXAMPLE 22.

[1] By permission of Messrs. Ricordi.

(From Coda of Rhapsody, No. II, Liszt.)[1]

EXAMPLE 23.

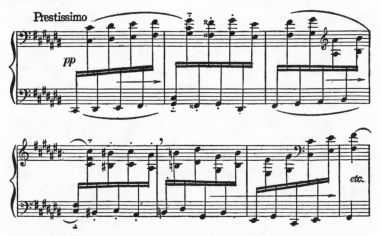

It is of no use trying to correct the playing of wrong notes **Wrong bass** or "split" notes merely by telling the pupil to be "more **notes — and** careful" — this may happen to have some result, or it may **other notes.** simply make the pupil more nervous. The only true correction is always to point out the *cause* of the fault. In case of passages lying under the fingers, or passages divided between the hands this cause may be found in neglect of that law of "Resting" on the keyboard which should render all such passages really continuous, physically on the keyboard.[2] But in the case of skips and bass notes an additional cause of error may occur:

Such wrong notes often arise from a *non-remembrance* of what should be the right notes, at the moment. The fault here arises from a totally wrong musical outlook. First of

---

[1] In this last illustration *both* hands should remain in contact with the keyboard, at least so long as the passage remains *pianissimo*.

[2] Refer to page 51.

all, note that you should always think the music from the
bass upwards, and *not from the treble downwards*, and
secondly, note that you cannot recall a *mentally-detached*
bass note any more than you can recall or remember any
other fact or circumstance, *if you detach it from its
memory-suggestions*. The only true correction of such
bass-note *guessing* (and failing) is therefore to insist on
the *musical-succession* of the basses being always noticed
and noted. Here again, as everywhere else, you see the
fact of PROGRESSION faces us; here it is the progression of
each sound from and to its neighbouring one which must
be noted, and thus fixed in the memory — the only way in
which any sounds can be memorised musically. The basses,
in playing, must therefore be thought as such successions,
and not as a wild "grabbing" into unknown space (downwards from the melody) — in any case a proceeding totally
against all laws of Key-treatment! (Refer to pp. 41–44,
"On Memorising.")

Progression in its larger swings. We have now seen how the idea of progression will help
us to understand the nature of Phrasing — the very life of
music; and how we cannot accurately "place" even the
inside notes of a Pulse (i. e., the notes between two pulse-
throbs) unless we constantly insist upon the keen realisation
of this element of "towardness" or "onwardness" (as one
may aptly term it) and further, that it still applies when
figures and phrases have unaccented endings.[1]

A warning against purely mechanical "scanning." [1] In attempting thus to "scan" or analyse the structure of the Music
one must, however, take care not to fall into the error of doing this
mechanically — solely by rule. So far from doing this, one must always
allow one's judgement to be swayed by the feeling to be conveyed — else
the result may after all be totally unmusical.

For instance, the rule is, that in a full close the tonic chord falls on the
more accented portion of the bar. It is a rule with many exceptions, but
it has led certain one-sided musicians totally to mis-scan Music; for

But not only must one think "towards" pulse, and towards phrase-climax, one must also think towards the greater crisis-points of the larger Shape-outlines, for the same law applies with equal rigour in the performance of the larger ideas of Shape and Form. Continuity in performance (and in composition) still depends on the same principle, carried out however on a larger scale. That is, we must always have a continuous travelling towards well-noted musical land-marks, and the proportions of the smaller details of movement must nevertheless, all the time, be strictly subservient to those *larger outlines*, themselves wrought by this constant principle of progression.

instance I have seen the Scherzo of Beethoven's Sonata, Op. 28, made to consist of four-bar phrases with the accent on the *last* bar, the tonic chord! See Exp. 24, at *b*:

EXAMPLE 24.

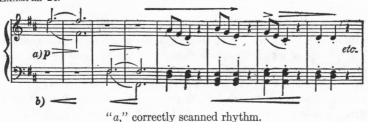

"*a*," correctly scanned rhythm.

"*b*," incorrectly scanned rhythm.

As a matter of fact, the true accentuation here lies just the opposite way — the dominant in the cadence each time carrying the accent, see "*a*." It is this very "contrariness" of its harmonies which forms the basis of the fun and humour of the movement. The proof of the correctness of this scanning lies in the last octave of the piece, for this is the long deferred resolution of the preceding cadences (so comically against-the-grain) it is the solution of the rhythmical riddle, since this octave cannot be construed as a syncopation. Whereas it would have to be so considered in the fallacious reading alluded to.

Indeed, in a really largely laid-out movement, such as we find with Beethoven, or with Tschaikovsky, we must often be content almost to gloss-over quite interesting points of expression-detail, so that we may not risk blurring the clearness of the large designs of these masters.[1]

To keep the *whole* in view is a question of memory.   Now, success in this respect (to keep the outlines clear) in the end resolves itself purely into a question of — MEMORY. Whether we are laying out a large movement, or a small one, it is absolutely essential that we should vividly *remember* the exact proportion of *musical importance* attaching to each of its component sections and climaxes, to its variously contrasting subjects, sentences, phrases, ideas, down to the actual importance of *each note* employed.

Only by such perfect *memory* of all its constituents can we hope to produce a musical picture perfect in its perspective, perfect in its outlines — perfect as a WHOLE.[2]

---

[1] Certainly, in a measure, the same care is required in works of smaller calibre, although it is easier to keep Outline in view in a short movement. The process of giving due proportion to the various sections of a large design and to the details of a small movement does however not really differ in principle from the process of giving a single phrase correctly.

Thinking of the " whole" expounded.   [2] In "thinking of the whole" this must not be misunderstood to mean that one *should be aware* of the whole piece all the time — at one time — that is absurd and impossible. Again, when we realise that we "*must think of every note*," this does not mean that we must think of all the notes of the whole, all at one time, that is equally absurd.

What all this means is, that in thinking of each note *as we come to it*, we may recognise and remember what its importance is relatively to the picture as a Whole; we must remember the proportionate "value" of each phrase, each bar, each note at the moment we are engaged in reproducing it, and feeling it. In other words, we must have an accurate *memory* of the "value" of each note *relatively* to the whole — from having recognised what is required of each note-detail to build up that Whole successfully; exactly as we must recognise what value to give to each blob of colour in painting a picture, if the result is to be harmonious;

This kind of memory is, indeed, the hardest task of the player — and I think it really is harder in our art than in any other.

But although this is the most difficult thing to learn — this necessity of constantly keeping in mind the Whole — the teacher nevertheless must unremittingly insist on the pupil attempting this task, from his veriest beginnings in the simplest music. For this attitude is the only correct one in Performance, just as it is also the only correct one in Composition, in Painting, Sculpture and in fact in all the arts. It is an attitude obviously in total antagonism to that *"doing of details for their own sake"* which I have already animadverted upon.

Thus we come back to the old truism — that we must never allow ourselves to apply the Means of expression for their own sake, but always for the sake of expressing something seen or felt . . . . not Doing for the sake of Doing, but always Doing only for the sake of something *beautiful* which we are perceiving at that moment.[1]

and this recognition of the constituent values can only be derived from an accurate memory of the Whole of these constituents, each one, as we come to it.

[1] Discussion of this necessity of attending to Shape, whether in play- **Perception** ing or composing — and incidentally also *when we are listening* — here **of a new** tempts me to a rather wide digression. We all know, or should know, **composition.** how extremely difficult it is for us to take in a new musical work, how we must hear it more than once before we can really see it — indeed, must hear it many times before we can really perceive its sense, especially if it is a work of any serious musical import.

Now we shall find, that really to perceive a *new* work at one hearing is not at all a matter of difficulty, but is one of *sheer impossibility* — sheer physical and psychical impossibility. The ground we have just gone over yields us the explanation of this fact.

In viewing a picture which is new to us, we cannot realise what it means until we perceive the relationships of its various parts; we cannot perceive its general shape, nor the meaning of its details, except by *comparing* its various portions or constituents.

Necessarily, this implies that our eyes must run over its various outlines *again and again*, until the rapidly gained *memory* of these details thus enables us to form a conception of the Whole.

In comparison with this process of perception, how extreme is the disadvantage under which a new *musical* work is compelled to make its first appeal to the public ear! Without our knowing what is going to happen, the musical picture is unrolled before our mind at *one single glance!* It is gradually unrolled and obscured again, beginning at one corner and finishing at the other extreme corner.

Now, if it be a good composition, it is so on condition that the first bar (and every subsequent bar) is in perfect relationship to every other bar of the piece — even those bars as yet *unheard*. But as we cannot perceive these relationships at a first hearing, we cannot possibly realise the meaning of the major portion of the piece, however quick our perceptions, since we cannot have any notion what the *unheard* portions are going to be until they have actually been presented *at least once* to our ears. That is, we cannot possibly perceive the various relationships of the details of Shape and Progression of a piece until we have had the opportunity of *at least once* hearing all and every part of it, seeing that the earlier portions can only derive their true significance from the balance given them by the later portions.

Here we clearly see *why* it is that a new musical work, even of the highest merit — or because of that — takes so long before it is accepted. In the case of lengthy works, there is no remedy available; it is not practicable to repeat a "Götterdämmerung" several times in one evening, even were a hearer capable of enjoying the process, and so one must trust to the audience taking the trouble to study such huge works before trying to appreciate an actual "first performance."

But in the case of *short* instrumental or vocal works of serious content, given for the first time in public, I do seriously put forward and plead for the adoption of the custom of an immediate repetition of them; such works should be performed at least twice in immediate succession. This would give worthy new music a far better chance of being accepted forthwith.

The old masters unconsciously felt this, when, in their Sonata movements, they insisted on repeating all the subject-matter, before proceeding to its amplification.

A musical work of serious import does not consist of a mere succession of surprise-shocks to the musical ear, although there is also a demand and place (happily limited) for such form of nerve-excitement or sensation-mongery in music. The real backbone of any musical work, deserving the name of *composition*, is (and ever will be) its Shapeliness, its architecture, its emotional and rhythmical continuity and strength; and this element must necessarily largely remain hidden from us, when, at a first performance, we are compelled to go forward step by step in the dark — not having traversed the ground previously with our musical eyes.

ADDITIONAL NOTE

Much bad playing, stumbling and stuttering, often arises merely **The cause of** from a non-realisation of the fact that all memorising, whatever its nature, **stammering** can only be achieved by impressing upon our mind the requisite and **unmusically.** correct *progressions*, sequences, continuities, or chains of succession of the music in all its details.

The teacher must therefore never allow a pupil to try to "correct" a fault, whether slip of the finger, wrong note, wrong time, tone or duration, by his playing the right effect *after* the wrong one.

It must be made plain that so far from being a correction, such proceeding is indeed *un*-practice. By playing the right note in succession after the wrong one we tend to impress a totally wrong *succession* upon our minds, and shall therefore risk repeating the blunder and its supposed correction the very next time we play the passage; and if we repeat it we shall be a good way on towards *ensuring* a stumble or stutter at that place.

The only true correction is to substitute the *correct succession* of sounds — to go back and *move across* the damaged place while carefully omitting the hiatus.

SECTION III

THE ELEMENT OF RUBATO

Tempo-con-
tinuity, why
necessary. ONE cause of the failure of the inexperienced to keep in
view the *whole* of a piece (while trying to be careful of its
details) lies in their non-realisation of the fact already insisted upon: that there must always be *continuity in the
tempo* if the course of the piece is to remain unbroken.

Remember, every time you change the *tempo*, your listener
has to start afresh with you, and has to readjust himself to
the new *tempo*. This engenders a complete disorganisation
of the piece, if it is a continuous composition; and if this
varying of the *tempo* is persisted in, not only does it lead
to discomfort, but to positive irritation, although the listener
may remain unaware of the actual *cause* of his troubles.

A simple cure in this case is to make your pupil walk
round the room several times, and to insist on his suddenly
altering his gait-tempo every few steps. This will make
him look and feel such a lunatic, that he will remember the
lesson for the rest of his days.

Continuity
also depends
on tonal and
emotional
planning-out. Continuity in performance, of course, does not depend
solely on obedience to this law of *continuity of tempo;* it
depends also upon the due planning-out of the Tone-values,
and upon the correct planning-out of the emotional stress
of the piece.

In this planning-out a gradual increase and decrease
of *tempo* itself may often help as well as such variations
applied to tone-differences. But this leads me to the discussion of a detail of expression which, while it is one of the

60

most powerful and potent, is at the same time one of the least understood. And it is one which is most rarely taught correctly (even when the attempt is made) since it involves a principle believed to be mysterious, although its comprehension is perfectly simple. I allude to THE PRINCIPLE OF RUBATO.[1]

Indeed, it is no exaggeration to say, that Rubato is generally quite misunderstood, even by those who may themselves apply it correctly enough in their own performances. *True nature of Rubato, usually quite misunderstood.*

Often enough I hear of teachers who tell their pupils they "must not play Rubato." Such teachers find themselves compelled to take this step, simply because their pupils have not been correctly shown *how* to keep time, nor the real significance of Rubato; and because these pupils therefore play absurdly meaningless *ritardos* and *accellerandos*, in place of the required musically-helpful and true Rubatos.

Again, it seems incredible that any musician in his senses could make the absurd mistake of supposing that Rubato implies any *breaking* of time. Yet I know of a number of instances where quite well-known professors deliberately tell their pupils: *"You must not play Chopin in time!"*

[1] Since I first gave this lecture, an amusing case in point has presented itself. In a book recently published (apparently for the sole purpose of abusing my technical teachings) the author realises that there must be a *something* apart from tone-inflection, which plays a very important part in musical expression; but, wanting as he is in that very faculty of "analysis" which he so much deprecates and despises — that "rationalism" which he so vehemently girds against — he fails to diagnose what is the true nature of this, to him, mysterious Something. Hence he lands himself in quagmires of verbiage, in "telepathy," and in hibernianisms, such as "silent sound," etc. Not possessing this despised analytical faculty he, in his blindness, fails to run to earth and diagnose this very "rational" but necessary element of *Rubato*, as the cause of his supposed "silent sound" and "telepathic" effects! *Rubato is no mystery, it is neither " silent-sound " nor " telepathy."*

Of course, both these classes of professors are equally in the wrong — those who object to Rubato, and those who condone Time-breaking — and their teachings only prove too conclusively how thoroughly they have failed to grasp the true nature of Rubato as an important and all-pervading Means of Expression. True, their musical sense is strong enough to make them feel that Time must often diverge from a sheer straight line, but so little reasoning power have these artists (yes, they play quite passably) that they are quite unable to analyse what they, themselves, unconsciously succeed in doing in order to prevent this very "squareness" which they quite justly loathe; and such teachers thus find themselves at an *impasse,* for they cannot find a way of rectifying the musical chaos into which they have misled their pupils!

It really amounts to crass stupidity in the case of men who have worked at their profession for years, although it may be regarded as a pardonable sin in the case of inexperienced young teachers.

Ritardos and Accellerandos are not Rubato. Now, as I insist on the absolute necessity for *continuity* in the performance of a continuously built-up composition, and as this can only be secured by insisting upon *continuity of tempo,* it follows, that constantly recurring *ritardos* and *accellerandos* are inadmissible as a means of expression.[1] Nevertheless, in playing, we are often compelled to adopt a device employed in ordinary speech, a device to which we resort when we wish to emphasise words *without raising the voice;* for we are then compelled to give   *more time   to   those   words.*

---

[1] Ritardos and *accellerandos* (in place of Rubato) are often marked by mistake by composers who have not carefully enough analysed the performance of their own works. *See* Notes, pages 38, 71 and 89.

Herein, then, we perceive the foundation and necessity The true of Rubato: we wish to emphasise certain notes without giving rationale of
Rubato. them undue *tonal* emphasis and we then naturally *dwell more on those notes* — we spend more time upon them than is their natural due.   But, as continuity in *Tempo* remains inexorable the only way to reconcile these two apparently opposite requirements (those of continuity and time-leaning) is to *bend* the Time and not to break it.   If, therefore, we wish to give extra time to certain notes, we must correspondingly take away time from *other* notes, to make up for the extra time thus spent; or again, if we wish to hasten certain notes of a passage, we must delay other notes correspondingly for the same reason; and thus we shall be able rigidly to keep to our Tempo outline, in spite of all this Time-bending and swerving.

In fact, we may, and should in nearly all music, thus Time-curves *curve* round the line of an otherwise straight-on Pulse, but constantly
required. while we do this we must never forget the line's true position in Time-space.   An analogy can be shewn to the eye by contrasting a straight line with another drawn in curves or otherwise ornamented, since such ornamentation need not destroy the true basic linear progression.   *See a, b* and *c,* Exp. 25:

EXAMPLE 25.

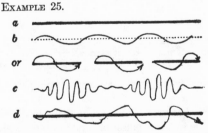

a, b and c in above example may be used to denote Rubato; whereas d is a *bad* Rubato, since the space covered on each side of the horizontal line does not here balance — does not "lead back to the pulse."

Thus in Rubato, we may seemingly disregard the pulse, or even the bar-lines for several recurrences, and yet we must never, while giving such Time-curves, lose sight of the place where the bar-line or pulse does recur *at the end* of such Rubato. We see therefore that Rubato-playing, so far from implying any weakness rhythmically, on the contrary demands a particularly strongly cultivated feeling for Pulse. Otherwise, when in a Rubato we are compelled to omit allusion to the pulse for several of its normal recurrences-places, we shall be unable to swing-back, or recur to it with the requisite accuracy at the end of such Rubato.[1]

Rubato in modern music.   No modern music is at all tolerable without the proper application of Rubato — and much of it. To hear a Chopin Nocturne for instance, or a more modern work played without Time-inflections is indeed (for anyone at all sensitive, musically) a horrible experience. Let me give you a taste of this, and show you what the *absence* of Rubato really signifies. I will play a few bars from Chopin's F minor Nocturne, first *with* the proper Rubato and then without it:

EXAMPLE 26*a*.

EXAMPLE 26*b*.

---

[1] Rubato, in fact, demands a Pulse-sense so strong and full of vitality, that it will enable us to feel a pulse (or Beat) unwaveringly, although its rhythmical recurrences may be so slow (or deferred) as to cover a whole phrase at a time — nay, sometimes half-a-page or a whole page of Piano music.

But while it is clear enough that modern music is quite Rubato in older music. impossible without Rubato, we shall find that most of the older music also requires it in a measure — although very subtly applied. Beethoven requires it less than the other older great Masters, but even with him it is not totally absent. Bach certainly admits it in a measure, and Mozart obviously needs it quite markedly, although subtly applied. We know from Mozart's own letters that he used it greatly, and much to the astonishment, mystification, and probable confusion of his contemporaries.

This leads me to a digression. I must protest against Fallacy re the old masters being unemotional. the tendency amongst some to imagine that because a great Master lived so many years ago, because his body has long been dead and buried, his music must also be in a sense dead — unemotional, un-alive and passionless. Could there be a more fatuitous mistake! Surely, all these great Masters were pulsating, living beings, *at least* quite as alive and fervent as we are, as emotional, as full of passion, as full of strong feeling and thought as the best of us to-day, and probably far more so! Indeed, is it not evident, that it is just because they had such phenomenal Enthusiasm for their art, because they had such phenomenal feeling and vitality —and reasoning power—that they were able to give us such masterpieces? Then again, the records we have of their playing, are they records of Mendelssohnian cold glitter? Do we not read just the contrary? Yet it is pretended by some, to-day, that it is not "classical" to put any human emotion into Beethoven or Bach! . . . Indeed, there are some signs lately that Chopin — of all people — is soon to be relegated to the realm of the cold and dead—and "classic."[1]

[1] But what a misunderstanding of a term! Should not "classical" signify that perfect *balance* of the emotional and the intellectual which is the very foundation of all true art? There is no such "balance" if we delete the emotional.

In giving emotional life, shape must not be lost sight of.   Now, please do not misunderstand me to maintain that Beethoven and Bach are to be treated in the manner of Schumann, Brahms, Chopin and Debussy! It is true, indeed, that the more shapely, the more architectural the music, the less ornately may it be treated. To smudge over the majestic arches, columns and domes of a really fine cathedral with tinselly colours and gew-gaws, is of course nothing short of a crime. But do not let us pretend that we can see the cathedral without *light* — without the strong shadows and colours, and mysteries — and rhythm — which light brings with it! As I have already said, in playing great works, works continuous and large in their construction, such as are Beethoven's, we must often restrain the impulse to colour each detail too strongly, lest we lose sight of the larger shapes of the piece, its general feeling and the majestic progression of its great proportions. We must play Beethoven not sentimentally, but we must play him with sentiment — with strong feeling, and dramatically. Let me play you a few bars of the "Waldstein" Sonata as I have heard them abused, and then with the correction of this mawkishness.[1] Thus: (A) with Rubato — incorrect; (B) almost without Rubato — correct.

EXAMPLE 27.

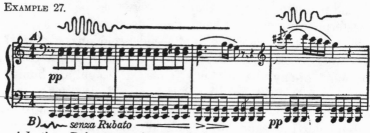

[1] In these Rubato examples the ⏜⏝⏜ sign is sometimes used for time-inflection (analogously to the tone-inflection sign $\prec$ $\succ$). Where the sign swells out the time broadens out. At other times a curve below or above a horizontal line is employed to denote the Rubato.

Seeing then the exceeding importance of *Rubato*, it be- **When to** hoves us to teach it as soon as practicable — even to the **teach and learn** child. It should be taught as early as possible: firstly, be- **Rubato.** cause a rhythmical sense can be acquired with comparative ease while young; and secondly, because of the extreme importance of Rubato in all modern music. And, of course, the child must begin its musical experiences with music of to-day and not of yesterday, for the average child cannot easily learn to think in a past idiom until it has had considerable experience of present day music.[1]

[1] This does not mean that we should feed his young mind on Freak- **The problem** music, nor on Flimsiness. Yet there is no greater mistake than to imagine **of music for** that because music itself has appeared in a certain order of evolvement, **children.** therefore it must be brought to the young mind in a similar order; and that we must, therefore, begin with the most difficult and complex intellectually, the most subtle emotionally, and the most wonderful of all the great Masters, Bach — a fine topsy-turvydom indeed! I must confess, for my own part, that I have still not entirely overcome my repugnance to and prejudice against Milton's "Paradise Lost," which was rammed down my throat long before it could be possible for me to digest it, before I could hope to see those beauties in it which I am quite prepared to believe may be there, but which are still closed from my vision because of the folly of my early teachers. Here, also, is the place to protest against the folly of giving deadly-dull and unmusical pieces and studies to children. How can the child learn to love music by being soaked in Non-music? Leagues of such waste-material, supposed to be "easy," are turned out and dumped upon the market as "teaching pieces" by the publishers — sheer platitudes, without a spark of invention or imagination or rhythmical life, saying nothing and meaning nothing, and such stuff is supposed to *teach* Music to children! No wonder so many look upon their practice-hour with loathing! This crime could not be possible, were it not that the average would-be teacher seems to be totally wanting in musical judgement, and hence quite fails to perceive the deadly-poisonous; nature of this commercial shoddy-material. For with a little trouble, there is plenty of real music obtainable quite within the ordinary child's grasp, and therefore stimulating to him — and also to the teacher; hence, there

Almost every child can learn perfectly well to feel pulse, to feel Time, if taught on the right lines — if taught from the outset to see (as I have already insisted) that music consists of progression or movement, progression or movement as regards Tune, progression as regards Harmony,

is no excuse for the use of material which is disheartening to and paralysing in its influence on both.

We must always remember, too, that the child is more likely to be in tune with present-day idiom than with that of a past generation. We have masterpieces for children written by such natural musicians as Poldini, and other foreign successful writers, such as Jensen, Godard, Ole Olsen, Theo. Kullak, Grieg, etc., while many worthy modern British names might also be mentioned, for instance, John Kinross, Felix Swinstead, Carlo Albanesi, Cuthbert Nunn, and many others. Some few exceptional children also are open to an appeal from the classics (such as Corelli, Scarlatti, Bach, Haydn, Mozart and Beethoven) but one should be sure of this, before immersing them in an idiom far removed from that natural to them.

If, however, such children obviously do enjoy the older classics, there is no reason why they should not be allowed to become familiar with some of the lighter works, or such a truly *modern* work as the Chromatic Fantasia — although, of course, no child can possibly fully realise the subtle feeling of such "grown-up" music.

In connection with all this, an interesting question was put to me at one of my lectures. It was asked "at the same time is it not necessary that music of the earlier writers should be brought before children as *literature*, and in quantities large enough to leave a definite impression of each great composer's characteristics?" The answer is, that each case must be taken on its own merits — what is poison for some may be meat for others. But *no* music, however good, should be forced upon anyone before they are ready to enjoy it; else we always risk creating a loathing for all music, instead of a love for it. One must therefore begin gradually and tentatively. Give the children music which they can enjoy (and that will probably be quite modern in feeling) and from this gradually lead them to perceive that which is in an idiom more difficult for them, an older idiom, or one more complex, and hence more difficult to master. Lead always from the simple to the complex in idiom, in con-

and above all things, progression as regards Pulse and
Rhythm. Obviously, it is also found quite easy for the
child to take the next step, and to learn to divide these
Pulses up into all kinds of details — always remember, details of *progression*. Now if the child can learn to do all
this — and can learn to feel portions of time *less* than the
Pulse, surely, it is only one step further for the child to
learn accurately to notice the recurrence of more widely
distributed beats or pulses — those recurring at wider
intervals, while omitting for the moment any reference to
the in-between beats — as required in Rubato.

struction, and in feeling; lead from the idiom of to-day to an understanding of that of yesterday. Of course we find exceptional cases, as I
have said before, of little geniuses of nine or ten who are quite prepared
to love Bach and ready to see much of its true feeling.

As to trying to teach children the "characteristics" of the various great
composers, is this not somewhat on a par with teaching the *events* of History to children, and expecting them to learn the lessons and draw the
conclusions therefrom, conclusions which history may possibly teach to
a few of their elders, provided such historical successions of events are
analysed so as to lay bare the evolution of the race, of institutions, of
ideas, etc?

Is it not premature to try to make mere children realise the "distinctive
characteristics of style" say between a Shelley and a Browning, a Shakes-
peare and a Milton, a Swinburne and a Rosetti? Besides, where is the harm
if they do not so distinguish for a time? The main thing is teach them to
enjoy and love Music. As to the teacher, that is another matter, the
various composers demand differences of treatment, hence the teacher
must understand such distinctions.

The two distinct fundamental forms of Rubato: (I) the "Leaning Rubato." To come to details: to begin with, we must notice that Rubato can take *two* quite distinct forms. The most usual is that in which we emphasise a note (or a number of notes) by giving *more* than the expected Time-value, and then subsequently make-up the time thus lost by accelerating the *remaining* notes of that phrase or idea so as to enable us accurately to return to the pulse. This return to the pulse must always occur at the most important point or note of the phrase — that is, near its end. Remember, this law is inexorable, we must always look ahead, and *come back* to the pulse at the chief syllable of the phrase, however much we may have swerved from it beforehand.

Rubato gives the strongest form of emphasis. Indeed, the very fact of our returning to the main pulse after having swerved from it forms the strongest means of emphasis we can give to any note.

For instance:

Example 28*a*.   (Nocturne F sharp — *Chopin*.) [1]

[1] Here we have a double Rubato: the main Rubato is caused by wavering over the first notes of the phrase, and the delay thus caused must be made up by hurrying over the first two quaver C sharps, so as to bring us back to the pulse accurately at the bar-line — the chief syllable of the phrase, with its resolution of the dominant harmony of the previous bar; and a smaller, subsidiary Rubato then prevents the subsequent demisemiquavers (32nd notes) from appearing square — this subsidiary rubato being in the form of a slight lingering over the first C sharp of that bar, while the time is again made up by a corresponding acceleration of these demisemiquavers towards the final note of the phrase, which thus forms an unaccented (or "feminine") phrase-ending. Played any other way, the phrase would prove totally unmusical. Both time-swerves (even the first one) are here most delicate and minute.

In the opposite form of Rubato (it might be termed *inverted* rubato) we begin with a pushing-on or hurrying the time. This we must necessarily follow up by retarding the subsequent notes of the phrase. This retard serves (like the corresponding swing-back of the *first* form of Rubato) to bring us back again, at the phrase-climax, into unison with our Pulse. And this phrase-climax, I would remind you, is *near the end* of the phrase. *See* Exp. 28*b*, and pp. 36 — 41, 70, 73.

(II) the " push-on " Rubato.

"Valse noble" from Carnival, *Schumann.*[1]

EXAMPLE 28*b*.

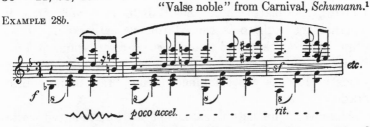

Moreover, these two forms of Rubato may be combined even in a single phrase. In fact, such *compound* Rubato is far more usual than the simple uncombined variety.

The two Rubato forms may be combined.

[1] Here it is well to point out that we must not allow ourselves to be misled by the inaccurate markings found in the texts of editors and of the composers themselves. Chopin, Schumann and Brahms, for instance, are constantly found to have marked *Ritardos*, when they have really meant the Rubato swinging-back of a rhythm after a preceding (but unmarked) accellerando; and *vice versa*, they have often marked *accellerandos* when they have failed to note the preceding causal ritardos. The simple explanation is that they have failed properly to diagnose the means of performance actually required for their own music!

Ritardos and Accelleran- dos in text, often found to be incor-- rectly noted. Rubatos.

Schumann, in his first *Nachtstück*, for instance, could not have meant a constant breaking up of the piece! No doubt in his own playing of it, he had noticed certain places where ritardos *apparently* occurred and he promptly noted these down. But he had failed to notice the *preced- ing accelerandos*, which are the *cause* of the swerve and balance in the Time-pulses, and which enable the piece to be perfectly continuous, while allowing a full portrayal of its agitated feeling.

The exact position of the return to the pulse must be noted. Another noteworthy point is, that in teaching Rubato, the only thing we can determine with *exactitude* is the *position* of the *return to the pulse;* for the actual extent of a rubato-curve may, and should vary with the mood of the performer, just as in the case of the analogous tone-curves. The actual nature of the curve itself is also thus variable; but not so the return to the pulse — that always has a definite and invariable position for each phrase.

The cause of the Rubato also to be noted. We should also, in every case, note the cause of each Rubato, the place where the Rubato is *begun*; that is, whether the Rubato is caused (in the earlier part of the phrase) by a "leaning" emphasis or retardation, or by a "push-on" or hurrying of the time, or whether the two kinds of Rubato are combined in the phrase under consideration.

Moreover, the actual extent of a Rubato-curve varies greatly, since we may use a Rubato to emphasise a single note only, or we may use it to give a graceful curve to a whole phrase as in so many of Chopin's works, for instance his Berceuse, C minor Nocturne, etc., or even to a whole section of a movement as elsewhere in Chopin, for instance in his F minor Ballade, Fantasie-Polonaise, etc.

Rubato allows a phrase-climax to be shown in decrescendo. Rubato, in fact, will enable us to make clear the climax of a phrase even with a *decrescendo* progression towards its climax; for, as already pointed out, it is a most striking fact, that the return to the pulse, (after having swerved away from it) forms the most potent kind of emphasis we can give to any note.[1]

In speaking of a Phrase-climax, it is of course understood that this invariably occurs either at or near the end of the

[1] Strictly speaking, there can be no Rubato "on one note"; but we may draw attention to a single note by employing a Rubato before or after it. *See* note, page 74.

phrase. This may seem unnecessary reiteration after what
I have shown to be the nature of a phrase— its consisting
always of a progression of notes *leading up to* a cadence, but
I have found it gravely and deliberately mis-stated in some
"instruction" books, that the accent of a phrase "is always
at its beginning"— than which there could not well be
anything further from the truth, musically! Possibly this
mistake has arisen from the fact that the first note of a
phrase *does* sometimes require a slight accent, to give the
effect of "good attack." Such slight accents are, of course,
in the nature of "cross accents," since they go against the
feeling of the straight-on progression. They are required
especially where the phrases and motives, etc., commence
against the grain (as it were) of the music, as so often found
in BACH, and the older Masters. Thus:

EXAMPLE 29.

But always bear in mind, no amount of such "attack"
on a first note must be allowed to mar or weaken the sense
of *progression* of the phrase towards its climax or crisis.[1]

---

[1] Most of the music-material of the old Masters commences on an unaccented portion of the rhythm. This rule often holds good even in the
case of apparent exceptions. For instance, the Fugue from Bach's
Chromatic Fantasia starts *on* a bar-line so far as eye-appearances are concerned. It is written in $\frac{3}{4}$ time, but the theme is truly in $\frac{6}{4}$ time, and starts
with a half-bar of this time; hence there is here no exception after all.

Various forms of Rubato illustrated: (I) The more usual or "leaning" Rubato.

We will now take some illustrations of these various forms of Rubato. First, we will take the single note emphasis, and as so many people imagine BACH to be Rubato-less, let us take his prelude in F sharp. The Rubato is here very slight indeed. Probably, if I did not point it out, you would not notice its influence — but then, Rubato-inflections should never be applied so disproportionately as to become noticeable *as such*.[1]

All means of expression must always be applied solely to express music.

The fact is, that *no means* of expression (whatever their nature) must ever be allowed to force themselves upon the attention. They must never be applied so coarsely as to become obvious as such to the listener.[2] I will now play the first bars of this Prelude, first *with* these so very necessary (although slight) rubato-inflections, and then *without* them, and you will realise how dismal and unmusically stiff the effect is without Rubato — although it is Bach!

The lecturer here played the first bars of Bach's Prelude in F sharp, with the proper (very slight) Time-leanings on the tied notes, thus:

EXAMPLE 30.

---

[1] Some even object that slight *Rubatos*, such as here in question "are *not Rubato* at all, but are merely a 'leaning' on a note"; these quite forget that unless every such leaning is *rectified elsewhere in that phrase*, it must inevitably imply a playing out of time. Every such leaning, therefore, necessarily implies a true Rubato, although of very slight extent. *See* note, page 72.

[2] *See* pages 79 and 120–1, and Section VI.

He then played the same bars without these inflections, showing how "wooden" the effect is without them.

Here it is well to call your attention to another matter, although it forms a digression from that upon which we are immediately engaged. Notice that the *tone-amount* itself must also vary with the varying lengths of the notes in such a passage. To be more explicit:

Tone-amount varies with note-length in uneven passages.

When you play such a passage as we have just had, a passage consisting of notes differing as to their time-size — notes of various lengths — not only is it necessary to treat it as we have done (giving slightly longer time to the longer notes, and slightly shorter time to the shorter notes than is their due according to the written text) but we must also apply the *tone-inflections* in the same way — the shorter notes must be somewhat shorn of their tone. In this way we shall more nearly approximate the general effect to that of a sustaining instrument.[1]

[1] For we find, with a sustaining instrument, such as the Voice or Violin, etc., that the longer notes are bound to impress themselves upon the ear far more than do the shorter ones, since the full volume of tone may continue throughout the duration of the note on such instruments, whereas with the Pianoforte the beginning of a note necessarily forms a far stronger effect than does the remnant of tone which we, as pianists, imagine to be a "sustaining" of the note — for even with the best carrying, singing-touch quality, there remains always a certain amount of percussion in every Piano-sound. *See* also page 110 on Phrase-continuations.

In a slow movement, the tone for the quicker notes is reduced from a high background.

Now, in a slow movement, these tone-variations should be thought of as being (for the quicker notes) a *cutting away* of the tone from the general tone-level, as in the Bach excerpt just given. That is, the main body of the passage here requires a considerably high volume of singing-tone, but we must relax from this normally high tone-level wherever the shorter notes occur. Listen to this Bach-passage once again, and observe now the process — the *mechanism* — of making a passage sound *un-mechanical*. I will play it slower, so that you may observe it better:

(The lecturer here repeated Exp. No. 30, pointing out the tone-inflections he used, all being of course quite *minute* inflections.)

To prove the case, hear it once again, given with all the notes of same tone value, and notice how ugly this sounds:

(The lecturer here once again played the bars in question, but without tone-inflections, after which he repeated them with the proper rendering.)

In a quick movement the reverse applies.

In a quick movement we have to do just the opposite. Here, instead of thinking the passage as of a large tone-level and cutting away (or lowering) the tone for the unimportant and quicker notes, we must proceed on a much lighter foundation, and must, in such quicker passages, *add* tone to this normally *low* tone-level wherever the accented notes occur; for instance the following, from Beethoven's "Waldstein" Sonata. (*See* Exp. 31, next page):

(The lecturer first played Exp. 31 with the requisite accentuation, then played it with its soft foundation touch only, then again with the proper accents added to this basis. He also gave as an example a few bars from his own Concert-study, "Bravura.") *See* Exp. 32, page 78.

EXAMPLE 31.   (From Beethoven's "Waldstein" Sonata.)

EXAMPLE 32.   (From "Bravura," — *Tobias Matthay*.[1])

Here again, the accents are superimposed upon a light foundation.

But let us come back to our *Rubato* illustrations:

Further examples of " leaning " Rubato.

We had an example from Bach, let us now take one from Beethoven. The first subject from the last movement of the "Waldstein" Sonata will serve quite well, although the required Rubato is here quite slight and subtle. The beginning of the phrase here requires emphasis towards the second of the two *G*s, while the further progress of the phrase towards its little climax must nevertheless be made clear. Now we should destroy the suave character of the tune, if we tried to show both of these points purely by tone emphasis. This would make it sound rough and raw, thus:

EXAMPLE 33*a*.

Hence we are compelled to resort to a slight — a very slight— Rubato. We must give a very slight Time-leaning towards and upon the second of the two *G*s, and the extra time thus spent we must make up during the next three melody notes, so that we may regain the pulse precisely on the *C* — the climax-note of the motif. Our return to the pulse at this point will sufficiently emphasise it without any undue tonal

[1] By permission of Messrs. Ricordi.

emphasis; and it will incidentally also connect the two short strains into one eight-bar phrase, thus:

EXAMPLE 33*b*.

For a *Rubato* of slightly longer extent in Bach and Beethoven let us take the second subject of Bach's Prelude in F minor (from the "48"), and the opening of the *Allegretto* from Beethoven's "Moonlight" Sonata. I will first play these, trying to give them their proper feeling *without the use* of Rubato, and you will see that it is impossible. I will then play them both with the proper Time-curves (or Rubato) and you will see how the phrases at once leap into life:[1]

EXAMPLE 34.

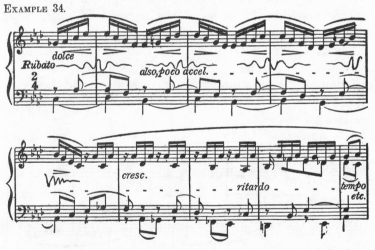

---

[1] The reader, in trying to carry out these Rubato and Tone-inflections, must always remember that they are to be extremely slight and subtle. They must never become noticeable *as such* except to the analysing ear. *See* the remarks on this head on page 74. Remember Chopin's illustration to his pupil; he first blew gently upon the candle in front of him,

Rubato inflections must always be carried out subtly.

EXAMPLE 35.

II   III   IV   I   II   III   IV   I

Example of Rubato analysis. Two bars of Chopin's Ballade in A flat.

As an example of a *Rubato* of similar character, but more marked, let us consider for a moment the opening phrase of Chopin's Ballade in A flat. How rarely, indeed, is this phrase given satisfyingly, or convincingly, even by the best players, except by sheer accident! This uncertainty as to success simply arises from the fact that the required Rubato has not been properly analysed nor understood. It is, therefore, worth while to analyse the Rubato here required, as it affords a striking instance of the supreme importance of accurate study and analysis of this process.

The *Rubato* in question occurs within the first two bars, but I will play four bars to give the phrase completeness, and will first play it without any vestige of Rubato, and then with it, thus:

EXAMPLE 36*a*.

Allegretto

mezza voce   *etc.*

and, making it flicker, remarked: "See, that is *my* Rubato," he then blew the candle out, adding: "and that is *your* Rubato!" *See note, p. 99.*

The Time-signature ⁶⁄₈ is misleading, it should really have
been notated as ¹²⁄₈; and the piece, therefore, begins with a
half-bar of this ¹²⁄₈ time. The structure of the phrase is a
swing towards the tonic chord; the opening E flat is therefore not a down-beat (as it looks in the original) but is an
up-beat — a *syncopation* in fact; and as such it requires
considerable tone and time-emphasis. This time-leaning
on the opening E flat is the *cause* of the Rubato, and we are
compelled to hasten the remaining quavers (eighth-notes)
of that bar, so that we may swing back to the Pulse at the
crisis of the phrase — the A-flat chord at the true bar-line.[1]
In this way we are able to draw attention to it without
undue tonal emphasis, while yet rendering clear the true
rhythmical swing. This chief point of the phrase is followed by a "feminine" ending, and here again a very slight
Rubato assists its rhythmical swing; and thus, you see, we
really have a *double* Rubato in this simple little phrase.
Here is another similar Rubato, from the same work:

EXAMPLE 36*b*.

And here is yet another such "leaning" rubato, but in a
quicker movement:

[1] The true bar-lines are here marked bolder than the false ones.

(From "Elves" — *Tobias Matthay*.[1])

EXAMPLE 36*c*.

For a somewhat more extended Rubato — a whole four-bar phrase with a time-*swell* in the middle of it — let us take Schumann's "Träumerei":

EXAMPLE 37.

Remember, such Time-curves must only be gentle wavelets, they must not be in the nature of earthquakes! *See* Note to Exp. 34, page 79.

Example of Rubato showing trend of phrase in spite of a *dim*.

To show you now how a Rubato will enable us to make clear a phrase-climax, or a main bar-line accent, *in spite of a diminuendo*, I will quote two themes from Beethoven and one from Chopin. *See* Exps. 38, 39 and 40:

[1] By permission of Messrs. Weekes and Co.

(From Beethoven's Op. 2, in C.[1])

EXAMPLE 38.

(From Beethoven's Op. 31, in G.[1])

EXAMPLE 39.

(From Chopin's Valse in A flat, Op. 34.[1])

EXAMPLE 40.

The three-bar rhythm of Chopin's *Andante Spianato* shows us how Rubato can make a phrase clear, in spite of its commencing with a cross-accent. As before, I will first play this *without* Rubato, and you will see how dead and stodgy

Example of Rubato showing cross-accent.

[1] Without this *slight* Rubato the phrase-accent cannot be shown here, since a crescendo towards it would be inappropriate; whereas its position is easily made clear with the Rubato swinging back to it. But this Rubato is again of a most diaphanous, gossamer type. *See* pp. 99 and 79.

it remains; I will then add the proper Rubato, when at once again, the phrase becomes alive — becomes vivid.[1]

(From Andante Spianato — *Chopin.*)

EXAMPLE 41.

Even in Beethoven we find exemplified this tendency to give a "leaning accent" (*i.e.*, a time or rubato emphasis) where the notes of a melody are syncopated; for instance, take the first part of the first subject of the Sonata, Op. 90.

Again the importance of scanning. Here, again, you will realise how extremely important it is always to scan each phrase before playing it. How often, indeed, is the beautiful swing of this melody completely ruined, simply because the correct rhythm has not been noticed. Although written in $\frac{3}{4}$ time, it is really in $\frac{6}{4}$ time,

[1] Note that this analysis of the structure of the phrase proves it really to be in $\frac{6}{4}$ time, instead of the $\frac{3}{4}$ originally written. The phrase begins with a cross-accent (or syncopation) delivered on the second bar of such $\frac{3}{4}$ time, and the true phrase-climax is thus thrown on to the first of the next bar.

with the accent always on the alternate (*second*) one of the original ¾ bar-lines.

It must therefore *not* be played thus:

EXAMPLE 42*a*.

(Wrong Accentuation.)

But it should be *accented* thus:

EXAMPLE 42*b*.

(Correct Scanning.)

Or, in place of such rough tone-accents, it is still better to make this rhythm clear by means of slight rubatos; finally, thus: —

EXAMPLE 42*c*.

(The proper reading.)

Here is a still longer form of "leaning accent."

EXAMPLE 43.   "Love-phases" No. 3. — Tobias Matthay.[1]

Rubato required to depict agitation.

This leads me to point out that Rubato is most of all required to enhance emotionally-agitated strains. Indefinite emotions, such as persuasiveness, longing, yearning, etc., all need for their due expression much "give" and curve in their Pulse-progression.[2] An effect akin to fog, haze or "atmosphere" is thus produced on the ear; for the details here become in a measure veiled, as in an impressionist picture. Much of Brahms, Debussy, etc., needs such blurring by means of the Time-swerve — and also by means of much *over*-pedalling and *half*-pedalling; while Chopin and Schumann are, of course, quite impossible without the constant application of such Time-swerves.[3]

[1] By permission of Messrs. Joseph Williams.

[2] Or, in other words, the *elision* (or omission) of the *closely-reiterated* Pulse-throbs, and the substitution of Pulse-throbs recurring at far *longer* intervals of time.

Always shapeful, however veiled the shapes.

[3] Such time-swerving, however, must be always in the nature of true Rubato, and must never be allowed to deteriorate into time-breaking and rhythmical chaos. Granted, that veiled shapes are beautiful, sometimes even more so than those of clear-cut definition, nevertheless it is the presence of Shape, however veiled it may be, which renders them beautiful.

The cry of some of our young tentative composers that Time and Key

On the other hand, when we do wish to express Definite- Definiteness, ness or Decision in Music, such as we find in all music which decision, best expressed is the expression of sheer vitality, aggressiveness, etc., then without we must make each detail as clear as a sunlit day. For the Rubato in- portrayal of such feelings we must avoid Rubato so far as flections. possible; and thus it happens that the music of Beethoven, with its appeal to all that is vital and fresh, and clean in life, and great in the Universe, for the most part demands almost the suppression of this far-reaching element, Rubato, except in the quite subservient and minute fashion already indicated, and except in the slow movements of his later Sonatas, where the feeling approximates so much more than in his earlier works to the intimate and immediate expression of self-mood — a characteristic of the so-called romantic school.

To make these points of contrast clearer, let me give you, Illustrations as an example of the first kind, the wonderful tune from of these distinctions Chopin's Scherzo in B flat minor, with its feelings of wild emotionally. longing. Without Rubato it would be impossible to make this rhythm clear — for this tune commences with a rising inflection, or cross accent. Instead of the written $\frac{3}{4}$ time, this movement is really in $\frac{12}{4}$ time; and the tune com-

are merely "the remnants of an old, exploded Scholasticism," of course merely proves that they have failed to grasp the facts which form the very basis of all musical art. Debussy himself, however, the strongest exponent of this new modernism, whose mannerisms they all try to imitate, has nevertheless a very fine sense both of Rhythm and of Key-relationship, although he purposely and skilfully veils both in favour of the exigencies of expression required by his musical individuality.

Another reason for the application of Rubato in such extremely emotional music may perhaps be found in the fact that agitation causes our heart-beats to vary — causes acceleration in the heart's action; and it would therefore be but logical to swerve and hasten our musical Pulse-beats when we wish to convey to the listener a sense of agitation.

mences at the half bar of this compound-quadruple time, thus: —

EXAMPLE 44.

To show how greatly *Rubato* does help us in such a case, it is well to play through the whole tune, first without any vestige of time-inflections, and then with these added, thus: —

EXAMPLE 45.

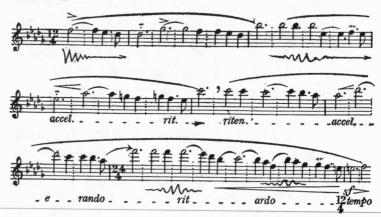

Now let us contrast the wild feeling here portrayed by the Time-swerve with an example from Chopin, where he wishes to be decisive, one might say almost truculent — the first subject from the Scherzo in C sharp minor:

EXAMPLE 46.

See how untrue this rings if it is played with wild Rubatos, as I have had it brought to me:

(Illustrated.)

The effect of the *absence* of Rubato here is heightened by the composer introducing this subject after a long Recitative-like Introduction of an exceedingly free nature.

As I find this is so often misplayed and strummed through like a badly practised exercise, I will play it to you as I feel it should be construed. Notice how the octave A in the final *Recit.* is really a syncopation.[1] *See* Exp. 47:   Mis-scanning of Chopin Scherzos again.

---

[1] Apropos of this, and the inaccurate notation and phrasing of Chopin, M. Peru "the only surviving pupil of Chopin" in an interview reprinted in the "Musical Herald" says: "As to his methods of composition, they were, contrary to popular opinion, most laborious. He had the habit of first writing down his ideas, then trying over what he had written at the piano and correcting it over and over until hardly a note of the original remained." . . . "When asked to put in marks of expression he put them in carelessly, never playing his pieces as they appeared in print, and marking a pedal at the beginning of each bar without paying the least attention to the sense of the music. His own pedalling was most extraordinary. His foot was constantly bobbing up and down so as to produce the effect of constant pedal but also constant sharpness." . . . "Chopin's interpretation of his own music was never twice alike, yet always perfect. He played with very sudden and sharp nuances, and frequent changes of time. As to what we call 'classical interpretation,' that had no meaning for him. Everything was beauty, and even a fugue he made not a dry exercise but a thing of genuine poetic charm . . ." *See* also Notes, pp. 39, 71, and Section V, Pedalling.

EXAMPLE 47.

Curious too, and unaccountable, the mis-scanning of the Chorale later on in this work, even by otherwise capable musicians. How often do I hear it played upside down, rhythmically! (*See a* Exp. 48.) Instead of, as it should be, *see b*, Exp. 48.

EXAMPLE 48.

One of the most wonderful Rubato effects is found in the Chopin *Berceuse.* I will play this to you, and you will see that the *Rubato* here often extends from the beginning to the end of each two-bar phrase, sometimes indeed being spread over four whole bars, and thus lengthening two short phrases into one of double the length. Each four-bar phrase is here transformed into one single bar — *one single complete pulsation*, or Swing of Rhythm; each complete phrase returning to the *straight* line of Pulse or Beat only once during the life of this complete phrase — at its rhythmical climax.[1]

Notice also, that while the right hand is thus at liberty to follow the player's fancy (but always strictly within the bounds of each complete phrase) the left hand, on the contrary, in the meantime keeps almost perfectly straight time all through the piece — with almost accurate reiterations of the three beats of each bar.

(The lecturer here played Chopin's Berceuse.)

So far, these examples have been in the more frequent form of Rubato, viz.: that beginning with an extra expenditure of time, which is subsequently balanced by an *acceller-ando* back to the beat near the end of the motif or phrase. We will now take some examples of the opposite, or "inverted" form of Rubato, wherein we commence by pushing-on or hastening the time, and subsequently return to our true pulse, by a proportionate slowing-up or retardation towards the end of the phrase, etc. This device is particularly required where Agitation is to be expressed. *See* Examples 49 to 56:

Illustrations of Rubato continued: (II) the push-on or inverted Rubato.

From Beethoven's, Op. 31, in D minor.

EXAMPLE 49.

(a) This sign ‿ꓥ‿ denotes a "half-pedalling" effect. *See* Section V.

[1] Such instances of long Rubatos — and longer ones — abound in the works of Chopin and Schumann, and more recent writers.

EXAMPLE 50.   Chopin's Etude in E.[1]

Episode from Chopin's Ballade in G minor.

EXAMPLE 51.

[1] The dotted bar-lines here are Chopin's; they are quite misleading, and the proper bar-lines and "scanning" are here indicated by ordinary bar-lines.

This really begins with a *half-bar* of $\frac{12}{4}$ time.

Chopin's Nocturne in G minor.

EXAMPLE 52.

Second subject from Schumann's Sonata in G minor.

Example 53a.

Episode from the last movement of same Sonata.

Example 53b.

Nocturne from York Bowen's "Miniature Suite," No. 1.[1]

Example 54.

[1] By permission of the composer (Avison Edition).

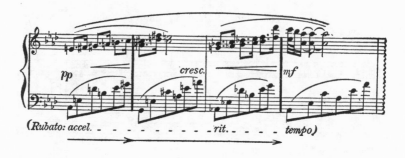

(Rubato: accel. - - - - - - - - - - - rit. - - - - tempo)

EXAMPLE 55a.

Chopin's Mazurka in F sharp minor. (Op. 59).

Rubato: rit. - - accel. poco a poco - - - - - - - - rit. - - - tempo
(Really one single "pulse" of eight ♩.s in duration)

Here we have an eight-bar Rubato, and the trio of the same Mazurka shows us how two-bar phrases, or motifs, etc., can be bound together into one four-bar phrase, thus:

EXAMPLE 55b.

The vertical arrows here denote the *only* places where the written rhythm really coincides with the *played* "Time-spot"—all the remaining bars and beats are off the *straight-on* line of beats.

Another, and to my mind very striking instance of this form of Rubato, is found in the second strain of the second subject of Chopin's Sonata in B flat minor. The whole of these eight bars should be played without any recurrence to the *straight-on* line of Pulse till the resolution of this strain, which occurs upon the first note of the repetition of the first strain of the subject, at the forte; thus:

EXAMPLE 56.

This complete sentence consists therefore of one single incomplete *long* bar of $\frac{12}{1}$ time, finishing at *f*, and commencing on the fifth beat of this long bar.

These two fundamental forms of Rubato are also often found in close combination, but the rules just given apply with equal force; for we must always arrange to arrive "home" upon the pulse at the climax of the phrase, or

Examples of the combination of the two forms of Rubato.

section, or "motif" as the case may be. For instance, the first strain of the Episode from Chopin's G minor Ballade which I quoted recently is a case in point, for it really needs such a combination of both forms of Rubato within its short life. Refer to Exp. 51 on page 93.

Another very definite and yet closely condensed example of such *compound-rubato*, within the compass of one short phrase, I feel in the opening bars of Brahms' Intermezzo in E flat minor, Op. 118. To enable us to obtain the intensely poignant effect of this phrase, we begin here with a "leaning rubato," but instead of completing this as usual, by making a corresponding acceleration straight back to the pulse at the climax of the phrase, we must here push-on the time so considerably as to swing back, not merely to the true pulse-line, but *beyond* it, and thus induce a well-marked *ritardo* upon the last two or three notes before finally regaining the pulse at the climax-note. It is well first to play the phrase through, perfectly non-rubato, and then to repeat it, giving the required compound-rubato, when you will realise how these time-inflections really are part and parcel of the musical sense:

EXAMPLE 57*a*.

Andante largo e mesto

Again, this Rubato-curve must be given most subtly — a life-giving breath, not a scenery-rocking earthquake! Do not try to express *the rubato*, but use it to express the intense feeling concentrated in this phrase. *See* pages 74 *Text*, and 79 *Note*.

The March-like episode (or Trio) of this Intermezzo, with its fatalistic feeling, forms an instructive example of sheer emotional effect gained by the *absence* of rubato in this case, for this strain should be given with hardly a vestige of rubato; and the contrast of its straightness and squareness, after the preceding wild rubatos, is most striking:

EXAMPLE 57*b*.

As another very instructive example of compound Rubato, let me play you a few bars from the wonderful Variations from Benjamin Dale's Sonata in D minor:

EXAMPLE 58.[1]

[1] By permission of the composer, (Avison Edition).

Here we have a "leaning" Rubato combined with a "push-on" Rubato in one single phrase, and the *plus* time at its beginning and at its end must be precisely balanced by the *minus* time in the centre of the phrase, so as to bring us back to the pulse at the climax.

As further examples of compound Rubato, here are three from Schumann:

From Papillons (No. 10).

EXAMPLE 59.

tempo   *non rubato*

From Kinderscenen ("Am Kamin").

EXAMPLE 60.

plus:
minus: (*Very slight rubatos indeed*)

From Kinderscenen ("Fast zu ernst").

EXAMPLE 61.

Rubato: riten........ *accel.* .... *ritardo* .... *accel. tempo*

Riten.......*accel.*............ ....*ritardo*..........................*Tempo*

And here is one from Claude Debussy — his charming Valse, "La plus que lente:"[1]

EXAMPLE 62.

Modern Rubato examples from Beethoven. Even Beethoven understood the value of a true *modern* Rubato, in his later works.[2]

As examples of this, consider the following two passages from his Op. 110 and Op. 111 respectively, *where he has tried to notate* such true Rubatos: —

From the Adagio of Op. 110, Beethoven.

EXAMPLE 63.

[1] By kind permission of Durand et Cie., publishers and proprietors.

[2] So did Bach — one has only to realise the true meaning, for instance, of the Recitatives of his Chromatic Fantasia!

From first movement of Op. 111, Beethoven.

EXAMPLE 64.

Rubato shows accent on a rest or tied note.

To show you now, how a Rubato can enable us to show a pulse, or accent, even *in the absence of any note sounded on the pulse,* listen to the second subject from the last movement of Schumann's Concerto, and the beginning of his "Des Abends" from the Phantasiestücke:

EXAMPLE 65.

pocchettino rit. .... accel.....

EXAMPLE 66.

Rubato always in the nature of a curve never a time-spike.

Another point, self-evident enough, which is only too often overlooked in attempting to give Rubato, is, that Rubato must always be more or less in the nature of a *curve* — it must be applied over more than one single note.   Otherwise, in place of a beautifully curved effect (the very purpose of *Rubato*) we shall have time-spikes (notes actually out of time) sticking out all over our performance — spikes just as uncomfortable as physical spikes.[1]   For instance, I have

---

[1] *See* Notes, pp. 72 and 74.

heard quite a good artist-pupil play the opening phrase of
Chopin's Nocturne in G in such spike-rubato fashion in
her attempts to supply the something felt to be necessary.
I will show you the fault and its correction:[1]

EXAMPLE 67.

To make such a mistake seems absurd enough, but it
really was a most honest endeavour, made by a thoroughly
earnest and in many ways experienced musician and teacher.
It arose from the fact that she had not been allowed to
apply Rubato when she was a young student, and could
easily have learnt its true application; but her teachers
had discountenanced such supposed frivolities — because
they knew not how to *teach* Rubato.

[1] May I warn the reader once again to be careful, in giving the Rubato-
inflections shown in these examples, to render them all subtly — not as
gross, noticeable Ritardos and Accellerandos, but as gentle curves, quite
unnoticeable *as such* except to the earnestly analysing ear. *See* page 74
Text, and page 99 *Note*.

Always keep
in view
musical pur-
pose, during
Rubato-in-
flections.

Hence, later on, when her natural musical feeling prompted her to cut herself adrift from the miserable straight-lacedness of her schooling, she had no knowledge or experience to guide her.   All I had to do in her case, was to make clear the process really required, and that instead of a pause on the first note alone, a soft time-curve was required, distributed over the whole bar; and immediately, in place of her previous caricature of the Nocturne (or "affected reading" as the Music-critic usually characterises any fault he is unable exactly to diagnose) she gave me the passage with due expression of the feeling which she had quite well perceived, but which she had been unable to express before, purely owing to her ignorance of the required process.

Here again, the moral is, that everyone should be taught while still young enough to learn things easily, and should be taught everything by direct, logical explanation of the means of obtaining correct expression.   Only too often is the latent feeling and perception of a pupil left unexpressed, solely owing to such interpretative-technical deficiencies as we have just discussed.

SECTION IV

CONCERNING CERTAIN DETAILS IN THE APPLICA-
TION OF TONE–INFLECTION AND THE BEARING
OF TOUCH–TEACHING AND FINGERING, ETC., ON
INTERPRETATION.

I HAVE here expatiated at such length on the subject of Rubato, and its application in Interpretation, because I have found that there is generally such extreme vagueness and misunderstanding with regard to these facts. But while Rubato is, as I have shown, such an indispensable factor in Interpretation, and calls for so much careful and detailed attention, this must not lead us to minimise the importance of other factors, such as those of Tone-contrast (those of Quantity as well as those of Quality), and those contrasts of Duration, which, whether obtained by finger or foot, are also, alas, so often lamentably overlooked — a point upon which I shall have more to say presently, under *Pedalling*.

The importance of Rubato does not detract from the importance of tone and duration contrasts.

The necessity for the application of all such colour-effects is patent to everyone who has the least claim to a musical ear. It is surprising, however, how frequently this imperative requirement of tone-inflection is, nevertheless, *overlooked* by the inexperienced teacher, and this, although he may be quite well aware of its importance! True, he hears (or sometimes does not hear!) that his pupil's performance is appallingly unmusical — sometimes enough to make him almost shriek with the downright misery of it — and the more musical he is himself, the greater the

Lack of tone-variety often not realised by the teacher.

misery for him. Yet he fails to observe the cause of his misery, fails to notice that his pupil's performance is either a mere stumbling, straight line of tone — totally devoid of any inflections; or else that it is far worse, and is strewn all over with supposed details of "expression," which are all diametrically opposed to musical sense.

I find many a supposed teacher continually experiencing this kind of torture without stirring a limb to save himself, or making any attempt to stave off at least *some* of this very real and intense suffering, but instead, accepting the situation "as one of the inevitable drawbacks of our profession!"

Need of accurate listening and analysing again demonstrated. Of course, I should not say he "listens." Indeed, he does not listen any better than his pupil does; that is precisely where all the trouble begins, he merely "hears." He hears sufficiently to make him sick at heart, but he does not "listen" — *does not analyse* in the least what he is hearing.

Not to notice that the source of his discomfort may possibly be traced to the absence of any Rubato-inflections is perhaps excusable in a measure, since these inflections are comparatively subtle, and he may have been brought up in the notion that such devices must not be taught, are really "very sinful," and "only rarely" to be applied, and still more rarely so by children, and never in the music of a composer who has been dead for more than fifty years! But with regard to tone-inflections the case is different. Doubtless his up-bringing has insisted on the necessity of these, even with children, so there is really no excuse for his putting up with prison-like, brick walls of dull, uninflected sound, when perhaps, after all, only a little effort is required from him, to enable the hitherto "unmusical" pupil to supply the needful tone-inflections, and to apply these correctly, thanks to a proper teaching of the analysis of Music, and of Touch.   The Means and Laws of tone-inflection when thus taught, renders the teaching of Music no longer an extreme misery to the teacher, but an extreme delight to him, as it should be . . . not to speak of the revelation it will be to his pupils!

In this connection there is another point which is often overlooked by teachers.   They *do* hear that the pupil is not giving sufficient variety of tone, but they try to make the correction at *the wrong end*.   They try to insist on *more* tone for the accents and the *fortes*, whereas, all the time, the fault lies in the fact that the pupils never get within measurable distance of a true *piano*, not to speak of *pianissimo!* For instance, they will begin the "Moonlight" Sonata nearer *mf* than *pp*, thus: —

Want of true pp is mostly the cause of deficiency in colouring.

(The lecturer here played a few bars from the opening of Beethoven's Op. 27 in this way, and then with the correction; also he gave the Episode of Chopin's D flat Prelude, with its long *crescendo* from *pp*, in further illustration of this point.)

Or they play their accompaniments far too loudly.   Let me give you a few bars from Schumann's Concertstück in G, illustrating this point, thus:

EXAMPLE 68.

After this it will not surprise you when I assert that deficiency in tone-colouring is mostly due to *lack of low tints*.

When you give your next lesson, just bear in mind what I have said, and you will find that your pupils are everywhere lavishly throwing their chances away, and are *wasting* tone, right and left! Say that a phrase comes out dull and uninteresting (even with a pupil who is trying to "scan" his phrases properly); in most cases you will find ·the fault is, that the pupil begins the phrase with as much tone as he *should reserve for its climax*.

Make him cut away the tone at the beginning of the phrase, and at once the phrase will stand out clear as a cameo.[1]

After a long note, the continuation of the same phrase is often played too loudly. Another fault of tone-balance, frequent in passages consisting of notes of different lengths, is, after a long note in such a passage, to commence the *continuation with the same tone* that was given to the last long note.   In properly playing such continuation, we should take care to give the note *which starts the continuation* with no more tone (or hardly more tone) than the last preceding long note *is actually* heard to give just before that continuation is due; otherwise the beginning of the continuation will inevitably sound like the beginning of a new phrase, and therefore "out of focus."[2]

Cut away the tone to render certain notes prominent. [1] A similar fault is apt to occur when trying to make a melody "stand out" above its accompaniment, or when one note of a chord has to be sounded more strongly than the others. Mistakenly, the player tries to give extra tone to these notes, instead of *cutting away* the tone of the others, and thus leaving the unsubdued notes prominent.

[2] Remember, the tone of the long note *decreases* from the moment of its percussion, onwards. *See* also Section III, page 75, *re* the treatment of passages consisting of notes of unequal lengths.

Let me give you an illustration or two on this point:

EXAMPLE 69.   From the Adagio of the "Pathétique" Sonata.

In the above example the notes marked with a cross must not be played with the same full tone as that given to the last preceding long note.

EXAMPLE 70.   From Chopin's Funeral March.

EXAMPLE 71.   From Chopin's Nocturne in F sharp minor.

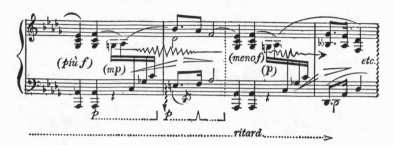

The indi-
vidualisation
and balance
of the con-
stituent
notes of
chords, oc-
taves, etc.

Another point with regard to tone-colouring, which requires constant judgement, is the balancing of the tone in chords, etc., — that is, the balancing of the tone of the several notes constituting each separate chord.[1]

Much variety of colouring is available by thus giving greater or less prominence to the upper part, or lower part, or inside notes of chords, etc. Every true artist, in fact, unconsciously chooses the colour for every note of every chord he plays.

Even in the case of a single octave, three quite distinct colourings can be given in this way; we can either make (a)

---

[1] Each note of every chord must indeed be *meant* as accurately as the note-details of every finger-passage. Do not play a chord as a lump of sound with the arm "dabbed" down upon the key-board, but instead, think of the three or four constituent sounds and fingers of each chord. *Will* the exact sound of each constituent note of each chord, its exact quantity and quality of tone, and its precise duration in each case. Chord passages, after all, are always "finger-passages" — in this sense, that the requisite fingers have to be called upon to do their work *individually*, each one in each chord, etc.

In this connection, the following is good exercise: hold a chord at key-*surface* level firmly (but loosely) by means of finger-force only, and *rotate* the forearm in the meantime both ways a few times, doing this *quite freely* while thus keeping hold of *all* the notes of the chord by the individual fingers — a capital "finger-individualisation" study. *See* also: Relaxation Studies," pp. 102 and 120, for similar exercises.

the upper note prominent, or (*b*) the lower note prominent, or (*c*) can give both with equal tone-amount; and octave passages, when thus differently coloured, have quite a different effect, musically.

(This was illustrated.)

To show you how much depends upon such means of colouring in octaves, etc., and the subtle effects thus available, I will play a few bars from the slow movement of Beethoven's Sonata in E flat, Op. 27.

I will play the octaves in the right hand, at first with *equal* tone for both the notes of the octave, then with the *lower* note more prominent, and then with the *upper* note more sung:

Example 72*a*.

I will now play you as another example of similar colouring, the coda of Debussy's "Reflets dans l'eau." The last two lines of this played with "solid" colour, would to my mind sound horrible. I prefer to play the right-hand part quite *ppp*, and in the left-hand the lowest note of the low chords more prominently — say *mp*, the upper notes *pp;* while the lowest note of the upper (trebled) accompanying

melody should again be rather prominent. You remember
the passage:

EXAMPLE 72*b*.[1]

Hardly any two successive harmonies are played alike,
in this sense, by a true artist or musical person — his sense
of *harmonic* values and progressions will unconsciously guide
him constantly to make subtle variations of tone-balance of
the constituent notes of each chord or harmony.

As an example of such varied chord-colouring, I will play
you the E minor Prelude of Chopin. Notice how the tone-
balance in the soft accompanying chords must be constantly varied, by *prominentising* the interesting features

[1] By kind permission of MM. Durand et fils, Paris, publishers and
proprietors.

of its harmonic progressions. This should be done, of course, so slightly and subtly as not to draw attention to this means of expression, as such. But I may have to exaggerate the point here, slightly, so as to make it plain to you.

(The lecturer here illustrated the Prelude in question.)

Still another point, often lost sight of by average players, sometimes even by those aspiring to the artist-status is, that far less force is required for the production of the high notes of the instrument, than that necessary to produce the middle or lower sounds. Such players fail to notice that the same force which will produce merely a pleasant *forte* in the bass of the piano, will produce a hideous shriek when applied to the high treble notes.

Less force required to produce the high notes than the low notes of the piano.

To convince the student on this point, show him how long and thick are the lower strings, and how thin and very short are the higher ones — the sounding part of the highest strings is only about two inches long! Hence, in playing a rising passage, which is meant to be of even tone, we must really play with a *decrescendo* of force, otherwise the highest notes will be of undue tone-value.[1]

Under "Rubato" we saw how we could give emphasis to single notes by a slight "hanging round" them as to Time — that is, by "agoggic" or time-accents, given either *before* the sounding of such notes, or *after* sounding them. We must however, as a rule, guard against a tendency *always* to give such Rubato-accents just *because* we happen to wish to make the notes of a melody tonally prominent in passages where the accompaniment is played by the same

The tonal emphasising of melody notes should not lead to tasteless agoggic accents.

---

[1] Obviously, it requires far less force to move a thin string, only two inches in length, than to move the mass of a thick one, some six feet in length.

hand. This constitutes a fault in taste (or technique) often met with. Remember, to add a *rubato* leaning to notes already glaringly emphasised by their tonal contrast to the accompaniment is only likely to lead to a very mawkish effect. Therefore, do not play Chopin's A flat Study thus: —

EXAMPLE 73*a*.

But thus:

EXAMPLE 73*b*.

Here the flow of semiquavers (sixteenth notes) should remain quite uninterrupted, in spite of the sounding of the *tonally*-prominent melody notes and bass notes.

There is no difficulty in doing this, provided the laws as to the rotational action of the Forearm are obeyed — and provided, that the notes of the accompaniment are played with those keys partially lowered before their actual final swing-down in the act of tone-production.[1]

[1] *See* the author's "Some Commentaries on Pianoforte Playing," (Longmans), and "The Forearm Rotation Principle" (Williams).

Now, with regard to the teaching of the *wherewithal* of Tone-contrasts — the teaching of Touch, Agility, Key-treatment, or whatever term you may prefer for this part of the subject, I need not go into these matters here, as I have been sufficiently explicit about them elsewhere — and at great length! It goes without saying, that during the teaching of Interpretation, I insist that it is necessary all the time to pay close attention, and to render the minutest obedience to those laws of key-treatment and laws of muscular action and inaction, which have been formulated in my various books on Technique and Touch.[1]

The bearing of the teaching of Touch, etc., upon the teaching of Interpretation.

Unless the teacher is fully alive to the bearing of these Laws, — and this, during every minute of his teaching hours, he is not "teaching" Pianoforte-playing at all, in the true sense of that word; for he is certainly not "helping his pupils to learn," but is merely *telling them to learn*, which is a totally different thing.

Command over interpretation implies command over technical resources.

The truly conscientious teacher indeed not only diagnoses every detail of Rubato-inflection, but diagnoses also every fault of Tone-inflection, every fault in duration, every sign of weakness as regards Agility; and, whenever any of these faults are traceable to disobedience to the Laws of Touch, he, in each and every case, explains these laws and processes to the pupil — while taking care in the meantime that the immediate musical purpose is never lost sight of. This he does, so that the pupil himself may learn to know *how* to correct such faults directly in the future — if he will but

Obedience to the laws of touch and technique must constantly be insisted upon.

[1] Works which had been overdue for a century or more; therefore the reader is here referred to the author's "Act of Touch," to the School book, "First Principles," and to their Supplement: "Some Commentaries on Pianoforte Playing" (Longmans). Also: "Relaxation Studies" (Bosworth); "A Child's First Steps," and "The Forearm Rotation Principle," etc. (Joseph Williams, and the Boston Music Co.).

take the trouble to do so. In this way the pupil gradually learns how every inflection and gradation of Tone and Duration, and Speed-requirement is physically producible, and producible with absolute certainty.

In this year of grace, in this country at least,[1] where such "direct" teachings have already become practically compulsory through public opinion, it is unnecessary to point out that this "direct" teaching of the essentials of Key-treatment is not only as important to the Pianist-student as the teaching of Interpretation and Music, but that it is really *far more* important to him. In this respect even Germany, which has stood still for so many years, complacently and with such thoroughness insisting on the interminable exercise-grinding and other monumental blunders of certain of her schools, even Germany is at last awakening. As I have already pointed out elsewhere,[2] healthily revolutionary writers there are now trying, with trenchant pen, to bring their country up-to-date and to her senses with regard to more common-sense methods of teaching Technique and Touch. These German teachings, although still tentative and erroneous in a measure, are at least similar in *tendency* to those of ours, now so long established and accepted here in England and elsewhere.[3]

[1] In Great Britain.

[2] *See* "Some Commentaries on Pianoforte Playing."

Knowledge of the laws of touch and technique necessary even to the beginner.

[3] Even with the beginner, even with the child, must these teachings of Touch or Technique be insisted upon. It is easier to learn aright in the first stages than later on, when various preconceptions and wrong habits of mind and body prove to be severe stumbling blocks and barriers difficult to surmount.

Harm only will result from practice unless the beginner understands at least the laws *as to the key itself*. For instance, he must understand that he can only direct and produce tone by a careful "aiming" of the key itself — each time for each note; that key-speed *is* tone, and that no

As with the beginner, so with the advanced performer, while you are teaching the interpretation of Music, you must meanwhile always insist on an accurate obedience to all the laws of Touch, for on such obedience does accuracy in Interpretation intimately depend.

True, later on in the student's and artist's work, many of these laws of Touch-procedure require but little reminder, provided they have been thoroughly mastered; that is, provided the correct actions have been made into unshakable habits. But there are always some particular points which nevertheless require constant reminder, even with the best players; and an unremittingly close and unswerving attention is therefore here required from the teacher, pupil, and artist. *Points as to touch requiring constant reminder.*

Let me go over these points; there are *four* such that seem to stand out beyond all others; two are concerned with the key itself, and two with the muscular apparatus.

With regard to the KEY: *firstly*, during performance, as I have just said, we must insist on that constant observation of key-resistance (before and especially *during* the key's descent) without which aspect of attention we cannot arrive anywhere near an accurate expression (or presentation) of what we may feel or see *musically*. With regard

further tone can be produced, once the hopper has fulfilled its mission; i.e., that sounds must be made through a purposed, felt and carefully directed key-motion, each one accurately timed. Even points of mere elementary knowledge such as these will save him years of time, otherwise wasted in the unlearning of wrong habits. Moreover, he cannot get much further, unless he also has *some* notion as to the function of Armweight, and its almost complete elision between the successive tone-makings; and he must, besides this, have a very solid understanding of the function of Forearm Rotation, and how constant changes in such rotary-activity are required of him — required indeed for each note, even when he grapples with his first five finger exercise.

to the KEY: *secondly,* we must constantly insist on accuracy in "aiming" each key-descent; that is, we must insist on accuracy *in timing the completion* of each key-descent, and without which aspect of attention, again, we shall lose all accuracy of expression, and also all Agility-ease, and control over Duration.[1]

With regard to the MUSCULAR PROBLEM, the whole here resolves itself ultimately into *freedom of action,* and the two points which for this reason imperatively demand constant attention and reminder are: *firstly,* insistence on a real freedom of the whole arm in all passages requiring Weight during the moment of tone production, and the real elision of all "down-arm" force (and excessive weight) between the successive acts of tone production — that insistence upon the freely-poised arm, without which, true Agility ever remains impossible. *Secondly,* insistence on the always carefully applied Forearm-rotatory actions, inaccuracy in which respect will vitiate practically every note we play.

Musical and technical attention must never be allowed to flag, while giving attention to the details of muscular education.

Here I must re-iterate once again the warning which I have so often urgently insisted upon, that in learning and teaching the wherewithal of Technique or Touch, the *purpose* of such learning must never be lost sight of for a moment.[2] At the Piano, the pupil must never, even for a moment, be allowed to think of a muscular action (however necessary) *apart from the musical sense of the notes he is sounding.* The necessary trend of the mind must always be: (*a*) "Musical sense tells me this note must sound *then,* and *thus*"; and (*b*) " I must be sure to feel the resistance of the key during its down-movement so that I shall be able to give

[1] *Vide* "Act of Touch" and "First Principles" for the various warnings given under this head, especially pages 125 and 126 of the last-named work; also " Child's First Steps " pages 2 and 19.

[2] We need not think of timing the *beginning* of the act of key-descent, but we *must* think of timing key-descent to *end* at the right moment.

the required tone, rightly timed "; and finally, (c) "the muscular requirements are such-and-such to enable me to succeed in this." That is, the *mental impetus* is in this order: "Time-spot — Tone-kind — Key-need — Muscular-fulfilment." It is but *one flash of thought*, thus built up. In the end, Musical-feeling and Intelligence must automatically prompt the taking of all these precautions, and it seems but one act of consciousness — this giving oneself up to musical feeling, emotion, rhythmical impulse and key requirements. Nevertheless, *timing* and *feeling* can never become an automatic act. It is always the act of consciousness itself which makes Music through these, and there is no real music without such, as there is no act of conscious thought without a *timing* of it. *See also*, pp. 33 Text, 41 Note, 57 Text, and Section VI.

Closely connected with the question of Touch itself is that of FINGERING. The older, and now out-of-date teachers of course placed an absurdly high value on this department of their work, and in fact seemed to rely on it as a cure for all ills — and some modern artists still exhibit the same failing. Granted, when your technique is inefficient, or your knowledge of its Laws is inadequate, that choice of fingering assumes a vast importance, since it then often means the difference between *barely* managing to negotiate a passage, and not being able to encompass it at all. With proper teaching, however, and knowledge of the *physical causes* which render a passage "difficult" or the reverse, choice of fingering is found to become a matter of quite secondary importance, since a far greater number of optional fingerings become practicable where the technical habits are good. I have noted the main LAWS OF FINGERING in my "Relaxation Studies," and in the special

The bearing of fingering on Interpretation, and the learning of its laws.

Fingering, also, must not be "crammed." excerpt from that book, published separately.[1] I need not therefore go into these matters here, except to refer to one point there noted, and that is, that great care must be exercised in Fingering as everywhere else, to guard against a mere cramming of "things," in place of a true teaching of abiding principles, and the nature of the facts concerned. Thus, in merely jotting down the required fingering for the pupil without comment or explanation, you are not giving him any real education; it is of no permanent value to the pupil to tell him merely to "put the thumb here," or "the fifth finger there."

Its proper teaching. No, instead of merely writing down the fingering of a passage, you must always explain *why* it is chosen, and *how* the choice is arrived at. The main principle which you must here make clear to your pupil, is, that choice of fingering consists in selecting such finger-*groups* which will most easily lie over the piano-keys concerned, while at the same time giving due consideration to the necessity of joining such fingering-groups each one to the next or preceding one, by means of the cementing action provided by the passing-over or under of the thumb and other fingers.

The memorising of fingering. The pupil will have no difficulty in *remembering* his fingerings, once he grasps the fact, that it is not *this* finger or *that* finger which matters, but that it is always a finger-group which is in question — either a complete group or an incomplete one. In a word, the act of memorising fingering consists in *associating* a certain set of fingers with a certain set of notes; this precisely defines the process, which is therefore an act of *mental association* like every other form of memorising.

Besides thus rendering it easy for the pupil to memorise fingerings, and thus to speed-up the learning of passages,

[1] "Fingering and Pedalling," London, Bosworth and Co.

such rational teaching will at the same time ensure his learning how to set about the CHOICE OF FINGERING for himself. This is an important point, since it is far more easy to choose satisfactory fingering for oneself than to have this done by anyone else — however expert the editor or teacher. Each individual hand has its own idiosyncracies; therefore, fingering chosen by another person cannot be so appropriate as that of one's own choice, always provided, of course, that one has acquired the requisite mastery over this subject.

For instance, in teaching the scale fingerings, do not tell your pupil where the thumb or other separate finger has to go, but at once show him that all scales consist of *two groups* of fingerings, a long one and a short one — the actual *lie* of these two groups being determined for each particular scale by the position of the black keys, and by the necessity of choosing the easiest positions for turning the thumb under, etc.

In the diatonic scale, for instance, we have the two groups:

$\overbrace{123}$ and $\overbrace{1234}$, these two sets of finger-groups being then mentally (and tonally) connected with the sets of three or four notes which they respectively cover, in each scale, the fingering and the notes of the scale are thus simultaneously memorised.[1]

---

[1] I consider it best to finger Double Thirds scales similarly in *two groups*, a long one and a short one; viz.: R. H. $\begin{cases} 2345 \\ 1123 \end{cases}$ and $\begin{cases} 345 \\ 234 \end{cases}$.

See "Double Thirds scales, their fingering and mastery" (Joseph Williams), where I have carried out this principle.

The repeated thumb presents no difficulty, unless one suffers from the vicious habit of "key-bedding;" and *legato* is less imperfect with this fingering than with the old-fashioned three finger-groups in one octave.

(The lecturer here illustrated this point, by taking the scale of E flat, and showing where the two finger-groups occur in this scale, the place depending not on the key-note, but on the position of the black keys relatively to the white ones.)

By thus learning where the *whole* finger-group each time lies over the key-board, we necessarily also learn the place for each individual finger.   To try to learn fingering in the opposite way—from the other end, as separate fingers first—is impracticable, and in any case we shall certainly not succeed in remembering *where* such separated fingers occur, until we do notice *where* the complete finger-note-group lies.

SECTION V

PEDALLING AND THE ELEMENT OF DURATION

WE will now pass on to another matter which is disgracefully neglected by the average teacher and pianist. I refer to the properly directed use of the Damper Pedal.

This neglect no doubt arises in the first instance from a totally wrong outlook as regards the Piano itself. Those who thus misuse or neglect the Pedal evidently consider "Pedalling" to be something apart, separate and distinct from Piano-playing itself, instead of recognising the fact that Piano-playing can only be successfully accomplished, provided we superintend the doings of our right foot just as minutely — and constantly — as we must the doings of our fingers at the keyboard. *Just as close attention required for foot as for finger.*

It is indeed no exaggeration to say that most of the pedalling one hears, even from advanced players (aye, even from concert-pianists) is just about as bad as are the smears and blotches which a child makes in its first attempts to paint a picture. While we are still mere babies, most of us, however, have sufficient sense to feel deeply disgusted, mortified and humiliated, when we see the colour-messes which result from our well-meant, hard striving to make "a pretty picture." *Most pedalling a mass of blemishes.*

Nevertheless, here at the Piano, we have fully grown-up people, sometimes even quite musically gifted, who in spite of all this, quite cheerfully misuse their piano exactly as these children do their brush, and make a very *quagmire* of sound, and notice nothing amiss — such is the force of habit.

125

I have repeated passages to artist-pupils and concert-players, pedalled precisely as *they* have pedalled them — with every vestige of phrasing completely wiped out by the pedal, in spite of a beautiful display of rising hands, etc.; and it has been difficult to make them believe they could have shown themselves so unmusical.[1]

Examples of bad and good pedalling. For instance, I have heard them pedal the A flat Waltz of Chopin (Op. 42) thus (see *a*, Exp. 74), instead of doing so properly in one of the alternate ways (see *b*, *c*, and *d*, Exp. 74):

EXAMPLE 74.

Not enough to *feel* the breaks between the phrasings clearly, one must *play* them clearly.

[1] As in speech, so also in Music, phrasing *always implies a break in the continuity of the legato.* You must have commas, etc., in your speech, and you must provide them also at the piano as a breaking of sound-continuity, else your performance will sound like "Flora Finching's" speeches in "Little Dorrit." Many players quite forget this necessity, and mistakenly fancy their phrases to be quite well defined, while all the time they are connecting each new phrase to each preceding one in an unbroken continuity of legato, either by a careless finger, or more often by a careless foot — to the complete obliteration of their phrasing. I have even had such argue with me, that their phrases *must* be "quite clear" (in spite of such non-phrasing) because they themselves "*feel it quite clearly*" — as if the mere fact of realising or feeling a thing sufficed for its expression to others!

Or we hear them pedal a passage with unbroken *legato*, instead of giving life-giving contrasts to it as in Examples 75 and 76, thus:[1]

From Carnival (Finale).   Schumann.

EXAMPLE 75.

[1] A mistake very often made even by advanced players is to continue holding the Pedal far too much, thus making an unbroken *legato* in place of that ever changing and contrasting variety of Duration required by most music.   They hold the Pedal wherever and whenever it can be held without producing actual harmonic cacophony, instead of being guided in its use by the ever-changing and exact duration-needs of each note. **Inadequacy of Pedal-discontinuity.**

The wrong outlook is: "can I *hold* the pedal here?"   Whereas the right one is: "can I *omit* it here?"

Strict attention to the duration-needs of every note demonstrates how surprisingly often one may and should omit or cut short the Pedal, to the betterment of the piece.

How pathetic is it, for instance, to hear a concert-player giving a piece, intended to be light and gossamer-like, with delightful lightness and brilliancy of touch, and meanwhile totally ruining the effect of it, and making it sound dull and heavy owing merely to a carelessly *continuous legato* given to all the underlying harmonies and basses!

Realise, that a gossamer curtain or piece of lace seems "light" to our eyes simply because of the spaces in its texture — the light-*silences* in it; and that lightness in musical effect is similarly wrought by the *lapses in* sound-continuity given to the texture of the music.

As examples play Chopin's two studies in G flat, and those in F minor and F major, and pedal the bass first in unbroken *legato*, and then again with as many air-spaces as possible in the harmonies and basses, and realise how infinitely greater is the effectiveness and beauty thus obtained. *See* Note, page 137.

From Concertstück. Schumann.

EXAMPLE 76.

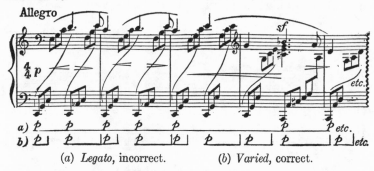

(a) *Legato*, incorrect.   (b) *Varied*, correct.

Or again, we hear what should be detached chords, *draggled* along by the pedal, thus:

From "Moods of a Moment,"[1] No. 2.   Tobias Matthay.

EXAMPLE 77.

No doubt, the fault is often due to the fact that even the best of us do so often allow ourselves to play *without really listening to the actual sounds emanating from the instrument*, although our musical intentions may be keen enough.

As I have already said here, a very great deal of unmusical playing arises purely from this very fact; for we may be *meaning* things, musically, quite meritoriously, but they cannot "arrive" unless we take the very simple and common-sense precaution to listen accurately *to what we are doing*;

[1] By permission of Messrs. Ascherberg & Co.

and this applies with redoubled force when it is a question of DURATION.[1]

Unless we have our minds constantly fixed (through our physical ears) upon the actual sounds emanating from the Piano, we have no inducement to let go either the keys or the Pedal — or to put this down.[2]   A simple cure for inattentive pedalling is often found, in merely insisting on the passage or whole piece, thus mispedalled, being carefully played through *without any pedal whatever;* close attention to the actual sounds being insisted upon in the meantime. It often proves to be a most startling revelation to the would-be player, when he thus discovers that till then he had been playing practically without really listening in the least to the actual *duration* of the notes played!

Indeed, far too little attention is given to the whole question of *duration.*   No one has pleaded more vehemently than I have for close attention to the inexorable need for Tone-variety — whether of quality and quantity; but while we are thus attending to this particular requirement, vital as it is, do not let us in the meantime forget the vast contrasts of Expression to be found in contrasts of mere Duration — contrasts extending in compass from the sharpest *staccotissimo* up to the fullest *legato* or *tenuto,* and not only thus far, but further; for the contrasts to be obtained from varying degrees of *legatissimo* (or the overlapping of sounds) are indeed not the least important of this wonderful element of Duration.[3]

Side notes: Accuracy in duration depends immediately upon accuracy in listening.

Value of duration contrasts insufficiently realised.

---

[1] Remember what I have said *re* " Listening," pp. 5 and 128–9, etc.

[2] How dismally dry is a singing passage when the pedal is *not* used as it should be, almost for each note!

[3] A good Scarlatti Technique, for instance (in the modern playing of him), depends greatly upon a full appreciation of the required nicety in Duration-values, just as a Chopin Technique so greatly depends on Tone-values, and nicety of Rubato-inflections — and Pedalling.

Let us now try the effect of a simple succession of sounds, first given with gradations of Tone-quantity only, and secondly, with gradations of Duration only:

EXAMPLE 78a.

EXAMPLE 78b.

Notice, that this last example is given without the aid of any Pedalling. As an example of the application of this principle of Duration, see the slow movement from Beethoven's Sonata in G, Op. 14, where we have such contrasts beautifully applied and particularly noted by the master himself; notice the carefully planned sequence of the contrasts:

(The lecturer here played the second movement of this little Sonata, so simple and yet so full of delicate charm when adequately performed.)

EXAMPLE 79.

Really, when one sees how often it is quite overlooked, one feels inclined to assert that variety of Duration is even of greater importance than variety of Tone itself!   Again,

Pedal-
duration
more im-
portant than
finger-dura-
tion.
the effects of Foot-duration are even more striking than those of Finger-duration. The sustaining and *mellowing* of notes by means of the Pedal is an iridescence hardly ever absent in a modern composition.[1] This enhancement of

[1] *See* note as to Chopin's pedalling, p. 89, *Note.*

the Duration-contrasts by the Pedal, however, is *not* owing
solely to the greater *resonance* thus obtained, as you might
at first suppose. . . . True, a somewhat greater resonance
does result when the Pedal is depressed, and for this reason:
that when we sound a note with all the dampers raised by
the pedal, the sympathetically-inclined higher strings are
roused into action, while the lower ones in addition give
the sounded note as a harmonic. Listen to the effect of a
chord played without pedal, and then with pedal:

(The lecturer here illustrated this point.)

The fact of more strings vibrating in sympathy with those
sounded does therefore certainly contribute to a greater
resonance, but besides this it also contributes to an actual
prolongation of the sounds, and consequent richness in the
Singing effects.   Moreover, when a legato is evolved
solely by the fingers, it is mostly a case of Legato or Legatissimo *between single notes*, whereas with the pedal *any
number of notes* can be thus rendered legato or legatissimo. *[Pedal en-
hances actual pro-
longation of
sounds.]*

Although I have noted some of the details of Pedalling
in the last chapter of my "Relaxation Studies"[1] I must
nevertheless glance at some of the chief points here:

I think it may be taken for granted, that even the most
primitive and antediluvian of teachers have now at least
some hazy sort of notion as to the nature and importance of "syncopated" pedalling. The reason of this requirement of course lies in the fact, that if you hold a key
down by the finger, and then connect that finger (in legato)
to the next note you play, a bad smudge will result if you
put the pedal down at *the same instant* that you depress
that next key. For, in a finger passage, you will necessarily
be holding up the damper of the first note with one finger, *[" Syncopated "
pedalling.]*

[1] "Relaxation Studies," (Bosworth & Co.).

Why it is required. *until the very moment* when you sound the next note with the next finger; therefore, if the pedal is made to raise *all* the dampers at that very moment, this will prevent the previous note's damper from descending and cutting off the tone, hence the smudge and cacophony.

For example, play a simple scale in both hands, quite slowly and legato, and depress the pedal for each note at the same moment *with* the descending keys, and the whole passage is badly smudged.

(Illustrated.)

Whereas, if you pedal properly (with the pedal moving down *after* the sounding of the notes, and going up *at* the sounding of the next ones) you obtain a perfectly clean legato.

(Illustrated.)

You see therefore, that in all *legato* passages, the pedal must *rise* as the next legato-note *goes down* — that is, unless the two sounds bear sounding together. In short, the *dampers* must reach the *strings* of the notes *to be* damped, *at the very moment* that the *hammers* reach the *next* notes. That is, the Pedal goes *up* as the *next* finger goes *down*. Now let us hear a chord-progression rendered Legato, solely by *foot-duration*. I will choose the very simplest progression, see A, Exp. 80: —

EXAMPLE 80.

But in addition to this unbroken legato we may have considerable gradations of Duration *beyond* legato, that is, gradations of Legatissimo — or an overlapping of the sounds, see B, Exp. 80. Legatissimo pedalling.

In a large room or hall, the resonance or echo always causes a more or less faint or incipient legato or legatissimo. But the difference in pedal-effect is even then quite marked — for the ear distinguishes between the resonance of the room and the resonance of the Piano. Let me play both effects once again, and you will realise the contrasts better: Echo-resonance of a hall is distinct from pedal continuity.

(Illustration repeated.)

To ensure your realising how this legatissimo effect is produced, and what enormous control it gives us over sound-effect, I will now so exaggerate this "overlapping" that you can hear the pedal *stop* the previous chord *considerably* *after* the appearance of the next one — and thus of course producing a slight cacophony for the moment:

EXAMPLE 81.

Numberless examples might be quoted of such "overlapping" effects, even extreme ones, but I will select one only — and a very beautiful one — from Schumann's Concertstück in G; I have shown the place by an asterisk: — Examples of legatissimo pedalling.

EXAMPLE 82.

And as an example of that rarer effect, the *extreme* over-lapping, I quote a few bars from my own "Moods of a Moment," No. 2:—

EXAMPLE 83.[1]

Pedal must rise fully.   In teaching these up-goings of the pedal, be most careful to insist that the pedal is always allowed to rise sufficiently, *fully* to damp the intended sounds, otherwise they will continue to sound in spite of the pedal having moved up — satisfactorily to the foot, but not to the ear, thus:—

(The lecturer illustrated this.)

Pedal must remain up long enough.   Also insist on your pupil allowing the pedal to remain up *long enough* to stop the vibrations of *all* the strings — including the lower and more powerful ones, else unwittingly, a so-called "half-damping" effect will result. This means

---

[1] By permission of Messrs. Ascherberg & Co.

that the lower strings of the instrument will continue to sound (will remain un-damped) while the upper ones are silenced.

(Illustrated.)

Sometimes, however, it happens that this "half-damping" (or rather, "half-pedalling") effect is actually required. It is required somewhat frequently, not only in modern music, but also in the older masters.   Now remember, when you do require such "half-damping," it is obtained by *purposely* giving the otherwise faulty action of the pedal-foot which I have just been warning you against.   That is, you must *not* here leave the pedal up long enough to kill all the previous sounds; to obtain "half-pedalling" effects, the pedal must be allowed to jump up only for an instant, and while this momentary touching of the strings is sufficient to stop the sounding of the *higher* strings, it hardly affects the lower ones at all, and we are thus enabled to play changing harmonies in the upper registers of the instrument, while retaining the sound of a low bass note, etc.[1]

Let me give you a simple example, where a bass is held through such changes of harmonies:[2]

---

[1] The so-called *sostenente* pedal allows such sustaining of any note or notes, while not affecting the other portions of the keyboard.   This pedal is used exactly as in the process of ordinary "syncopated" pedalling. The device has been applied by several makers; it is of course an extra expense in manufacture, which fact no doubt sufficiently accounts for its not being adopted generally; also, it is inclined to make the touch of the instrument a little more clumsy and uneven for the time being — that is, while this pedal is held down.   Musically, however, there would be a distinct advantage in having it on all pianos.

[2] A familiar example is found in the well-known Rachmaninoff Prelude.

Margin notes: Half-damping effects. — The "Sostenente" pedal.

EXAMPLE 84.

The ‿∧‿∧‿ mark in the Pedal line is meant to suggest the momentary rising action of the foot in those places — the "half-damping" effect.

Half-pedalling applied to whole chords.

Whole chords, low down, may also be somewhat similarly "half-damped;" only a small remainder of the full sustaining power being thus left after a strong percussion. It is rather a striking effect, but only rarely applicable. Liszt's Sonata in B minor offers us a striking instance:

EXAMPLE 85.

Cessation of sound as a form of emphasis.

Another point as to Duration, which I find is so often overlooked both by players and teachers, is the fact that we can produce an actual *emphasis* by making a large body of sound *cease* accurately and sharply on a beat or pulse. I mean, that we can call attention to a pulse-place (and thus give it emphasis) if, after sounding and holding a strong chord with the pedal, we release it quite suddenly, and

precisely *on such pulse.*   Take for instance, a final chord,
thus:

EXAMPLE 86.

We also employ this device of detachment as a form of emphasis in ordinary speech at times, when we wish to be particularly assertive; for instance, instead of gliding over
the phrase "Now⌣mind⌣you⌣do⌣this⌣" we ejaculate:
"Now! mind — you — do — this!" . . . We do not *legato*
the ejaculation "Lookoutacariscoming," but we emphasise it by a staccato "Look-out!" from the rest of the
shriek.[1]

   To show you how passages can be enhanced in their
emphasis by such cutting short of the note-durations, I
will give you the first entries of the Solo Piano in several of
the Concertos — passages meant to be as emphatic and assertive as possible.   I will first play them Pedal-*legato*, and
you will see how ineffective they are thus, and I will then
play them with the proper detached emphasis — by judicious
raising of the Pedal, thus:

---

   [1] Mozart said, "Silence is the greatest effect in Music."   Indeed, he
well knew the value not only of Duration-varieties, but the value of
rests.   We, now-a-days, hardly ever have the courage to wait a bar or
two in complete, striking silence, to enable the ear to look forward to the
next sound!

From Schumann's Concerto.

EXAMPLE 87.

From Grieg's Concerto.

EXAMPLE 88.

From Rubinstein's D minor Concerto.

EXAMPLE 89.

From A. C. Mackenzie's "Scottish Concerto."[1]

EXAMPLE 90.

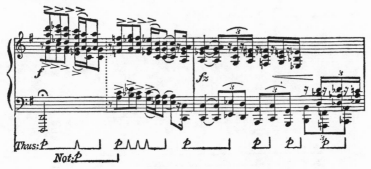

[1] By kind permission of the composer.

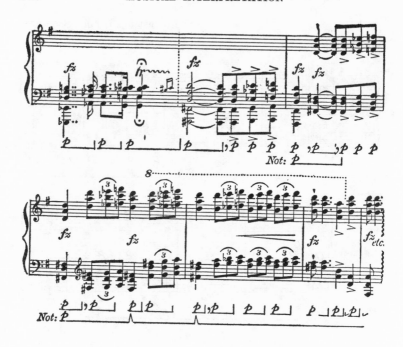

From Liszt's Concerto in E flat.

EXAMPLE 91.

Indeed, quite an extraordinary number of distinct effects can be produced, simply by careful foot-cessations, if only we give the requisite study to this important matter which it so urgently needs, and closely attend — and listen — to Duration *all the time* we are playing and studying, and are Teaching.[1]

Imperative to listen accurately and constantly to duration.

Let me give you a few further examples bearing on these points. For varieties of short basses:

Various additional pedalling examples.

From D flat Waltz, Chopin.

EXAMPLE 92.

---

[1] While it is not accurate to assert (as has been done by an enthusiast on his first beginning to realise the potency of Pedalling) that "Seventy-five per cent of good playing is correct pedalling," it is imperative to recognise that *bad pedalling* (and inaccuracy in Duration-values generally) will indeed only too easily ruin "75%" — and much more — of ones playing!

EXAMPLE 93.

From F minor study, Chopin.

To give the "feathery" effect to the little arpeggio in the right hand:

From Beethoven's Rondo in G.

EXAMPLE 94.

As examples of "half-pedalling" or "half-damping":

From G minor Ballade, Chopin.

EXAMPLE 95.

Remember the *Note* as to Chopin's pedalling, **page 89**!

From Albumblad in B-flat, Grieg.

EXAMPLE 96*a*.

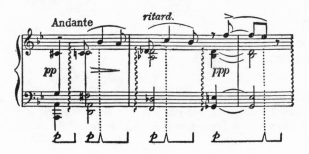

And from the same little piece:

Example 96b.

As an example of many similar half-pedalling effects required in Brahms:

Episode from Rhapsody in G minor, Brahms.

Example 97a.

The impressive effect of this passage would be lost were the Bass pedalled *legato*. Sustaining the pedal to the *third* beat would still sound clumsy; hence the only solution is to "half-pedal" at the *second* beat, and to make a complete break before the fourth beat, as notated.

Coda from the same Rhapsody.

EXAMPLE 97b.

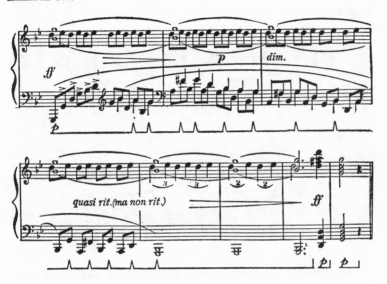

Chopin also well understood this effect:

From Coda of Prelude in A flat, Chopin.

EXAMPLE 98.

As an example of Cessation-emphasis:

Ballade from Op. 118, Brahms.

EXAMPLE 99.

Finally, the lecturer (to show varieties of Pedal-effect) played some pages of Brahms' Rhapsody in B minor:

EXAMPLE 100.

Listen both to finger and foot doings. I think I have shown you enough to convince you how imperative it is not only to "listen with your fingers," as the empiric phrase has it (and a very useful old empiric phrase it is) but also, that you must strive to "listen" just as accurately, definitely, and purposefully with *your foot*.[1]

It is not a complex problem at all if we only cease making distinctions which do not really exist!   Be it right hand or left hand, or any finger-tip of either, or be it our right foot, they are all but part of us — part of our body, why then delude ourselves into considering them to be separate "things"?   *All* are able to send sense-impressions to our brain from resistances experienced outside our bodies, and all must help in providing the required effects.

Evidently, whether we touch the piano (and act upon it) with a finger or a foot, it is always "*we*" — ourselves, who are thus deriving impressions from the instrument (the piano itself) and ordering actions outside of us (and within us) in consequence.   Why then have bits of "we," a right hand bit, or a left hand bit, or a foot bit?   Instead of all such distinctions, let us thoroughly realise that we must all the time be keenly alert to what our sensation-apparatus *as a whole* conveys to us from the Piano, so that we may properly order and *time* the musical and muscular *doing*. The sensation of KEY-RESISTANCE and the sensation of PEDAL-RESISTANCE, these are both but part and parcel of that single thought and purpose, summed up as "performing-attention" — and that means: *attention to Music* — THROUGH OUR INSTRUMENT.

Attention during performance.

[1] Foot and Finger together make up the musical effect we need, therefore do not let us separate these into distinct and often *conflicting* departments, but let them always act in consonance, indeed as one person. At the piano, we must know no distinction or separateness between our right and left hands, neither may we make these distinct from our *right* Foot.

SECTION VI

THE PURPOSE OF ART–EXPRESSION AND ITS RELATION TO THE INFINITE

The ever-present danger of forgetting the end over the means. COMING back to Nature — to the stillness of the country, to sky-expanse and wind-driven cloud, to the magic of the woods and the mystery of the starlit-nights — a fundamental truth is ever insinuatingly and forcibly driven home to us. There is a paralysing mistake which all of us are only too liable to make in our art-efforts. In giving the necessarily close attention to the wherewithal of Expression, be it in composition or in performance, painting or poetising, or in the teaching of these things, there is always this great danger lurking for us, that we are liable not only to forget Art in the doing of it, but liable to forget *what should be the purpose of Art*—the very purpose of our pursuit!

Brought back into close contact with unsullied, un-brick-poisoned Nature, that purpose reasserts itself in tones that refuse to be passed by unheeded.

The purpose of art is the expression of feeling. If we are impressionable — and we cannot be artists unless we are — we find that things in Nature and in Humanity around us impress us strongly, in various ways, and arouse in us vivid feelings, or moods. Now, the purpose of Art, whatever its form, is primarily and mainly the expression of Moods and Feelings, thus engendered.

If then we would be Artists, we must earnestly and honestly strive to do neither more nor less than to give

148

expression to such emotional states, moods, or feelings. We must use our intelligence so that our feelings shall be duly expressed. And if we do use all our technical resources for this *sole purpose*, we may possibly succeed in producing a real, living work of Art, which, being vivid, may in its turn impress others with a mood, feeling or emotional state — possibly of a like nature.

The attempt to write notes, or play them, or sing them, or to recite, or paint, or versify, *unless under such emotional stress*, can only lead to failure — sheer waste of time, sheer folly so far as true Art is concerned. "Nothing can only produce — Nothing!"

Of course it does not follow, that even if we do try our utmost to attend to the mood induced in us by Nature herself, by human feeling, *or by some real work of art*, that therefore we ourselves shall succeed in producing a real work of art; but we shall know, at least, that we are on the right track. The other ever remains empty Nothingness, mere pretence and hypocrisy— Artisanship maybe, but not Art!

Also there always remains the question, WHAT MOOD? — Art-moods which make for good and which make for evil. but that is another story! There are moods that *raise* us or help us to raise others, — moods that help us to live and think better; or, on the other hand, there are moods which have quite the reverse effect. . . . Thus we may have Art which is a mere pandering to self and morbidity, or we may have Art which raises our thoughts beyond the daily necessity (and struggle very often) of making our daily bread. Art, which may help us to see the great wonder of Nature around us, and to see how, in our own lives, we can be more or less in harmony with it, *if we but try*. And our thoughts revert to those real masterpieces of Nature-music of which

BEETHOVEN and BACH, for instance, have given us so many.[1]

Health and mood.

[1] The fact of our being at all "in the mood" to compose or perform is, however, a question quite distinct from this one.

After all that has been formulated as to the facts of *doing*, we are nevertheless helpless, unless we happen to be in such a performing or composing "mood" or humour — helpless, so far as the attainment of any really valuable artistic result is concerned.

True, a knowledge of the facts and laws of Expression and Technique will enable us to lessen the evil effect of "non-mood," and also such knowledge will enable us better to express ourselves during the stress of so-called "Inspiration," but the exceedingly exasperating fact remains, that in the end we remain very much at the mercy of our bodily moods — physical moods wrought by our precise state of health! The whole question resolves itself ultimately into one of Vitality. It is possible that we may be "in the mood" or "inspired" when the thermometer of our vitality is high, but we cannot be when it is low — notwithstanding what seem to be occasional exceptions to this rule, when a feverish state of over-excitement stimulates our imagination, and simulates the effects of true vigorous vitality. It is when our vitality-thermometer is high that we feel alert and keen mentally, find ourselves open to new impressions, and alive to the promptings of a healthy imagination vividly active for the time. But when the tide of vitality is at its lower ebb, neither can we assimilate new impressions, nor will our brain provide any. Moreover, these mental states re-act with redoubled effect muscularly. Remember, the "natural" state of the muscles is one of tenseness, not one of relaxation; this is the meaning of "rigor mortis." In order to *relax* our muscles we must use up vital energy. Take away that energy and they close up and tighten.

Thus it happens, when our vitality is at a lower ebb, that all the muscles of our body tend to approximate to the state of death; there becomes evident in them a tendency towards less promptitude and less ease in relaxation than obtains during our moments of full vital energy. Any gymnastic action or exertion (such as Pianoforte playing or Singing, etc.) which we may undertake under such unfavourable conditions of mind and body, will have to be fulfilled while the "opposite" or "contrary" muscles remain more or less active — tense and impedimental therefore.

Here we see why it is, that when we are not in a musical mood (i.e.,

Now, these thoughts can be profitably pursued still The nature of music, its relation to all-pervading rhythm and to the ultimately unknowable. further, and to good practical purpose. In the factor which all sane musicians hold and consider to be the most striking manifestation of Music, the very basis, the very life of it, we shall find a good foundation for the belief that Music is intimate with Nature herself. This factor is what we term Pulse, Time, Accent, that is — Rhythm.

It has been conceded by many that Music is the most powerful of the arts, that it is the art which brings us most intimately into communion with the Ultimate Unknowable in Nature, that it seems to be *the* form of human thought which brings us nearest to an overcoming of the very limitations of our Thought-mechanism . . . — that it brings us most nearly into contact with that which must forever remain outside the grasp of our Mind.

Now the reason why Music is thus the most powerful of the Arts lies surely in its immediate relationship (through Pulse, Time and Accent) to the cosmic all-pervading Rhythm — its relationship to the ultimate Fact and Being of the Universe.

Most of us, I hope, do recognise that Music is indeed dead as a door-nail unless the keenest sense of Pulse and Accent is kept alive and insisted upon by teacher, pupil

not in a state of general alertness) our Technique also is found to be unresponsive, woefully impoverished and nullified.

It is our vitality which is the ultimate cause of our seeing vividly what to do, our vitality again which leaves our muscles unfettered by their fellows.

If we bear these facts in mind, we can however in some measure lessen the evil effects of the muscular tension of a low vitality, by *inhibiting* the wrong exertions, by trying to be effortless, by trying to remember the sensation of ease experienced at more favourable times coupled with keen rhythmical alertness, and thus recall somewhat the feeling of unrestrained, vigorous rhythmical *doing* associated with our moments of bright vitality.

and performer. Sounds, however finely we may inflect
their tone and duration, signify nothing *unless* the vitalising basis of Rhythm is insisted upon — in the form of a
well-defined Pulse, and in the form of constantly-continued
accentuational GROWTH.

It is indeed solely through its direct appeal to our sense
of Pulse-throb, sense of rhythmical growth and Progression,
that music rouses us to a sense or feeling of *something vital
and alive.*[1]

Through this supreme fact of its manifestation, Music,
indeed, brings INFINITUDE itself within our ken. It is easy
to realise why this is so. . . .

Glibly enough do we speak of the ultimate unknowables,
Time and Space. But we do not always realise, that while
we cannot think of any manifestation of Energy or Matter
without the element of extension in Space, nevertheless, *all*
manifestations (whatever their nature, including those of
Thought and Consciousness itself) must ultimately resolve
themselves into manifestations of Pulse — or Extension *in
time!* Pulse—Vibration—Rhythm indeed pervades everything; and, in fact, constitutes *the ultimate of all that is.*

If we look around us, all that which we call "life"
exists solely by nature of this vitalising element of Pulse,
from Humanity down to the mere Diatom.   Again, if
we look outside that limited series of manifestations called

---

[1] Omit this, and music is indeed dead and useless — merely a succession
of "pretty noises."   But give it, and then with it, and through it we have
the strongest appeal to the very fundamentals of our nature — always
provided that the hearer is a Seer in a measure, and is not stone-blind
or deaf to musical feeling and human emotion. Thus we gain a vision, a
faint one maybe, but a convincing one, of the Something which is the very
basis of Nature, outside our thought and sense-perceptions. Such is the
wonderful power which Music can have over us — the power of opening
up to us a glimpse of the BEYOND!

life, and on a starry night realise the unthinkable, stupefying infinitudes of the star-depths, we become all the more conscious of this persistence of the element of Pulse, or Rhythm!   If we turn to a consideration of the various manifestations of Energy — Sound, Light, Heat and Electricity — again are we brought face to face with the almighty doings of Pulse, — Pulse, in the form of infinitely quick vibrations, still more overpowering in *their* grandeur.   Nay, the very *thing* we call Matter, the very substances which form our seemingly inert Earth (with all its metals, its rocks, and its gases) do we not find that even this seemingly "dead" matter in the end probably resolves itself into variously constituted manifestations of PULSE — the Rhythm of "vortex atoms?"

Here then, we are face to face with that One, Allpervading, ultimate SOMETHING — the vitalising, palpitating factor, which, although forever incomprehensible, is tremendous in its Almightiness.   In a word, we are fain to feel that we are here face to face with that ultimate, Unknowable Fact, or PRESENCE which the older Religions have with one accord recognised — which they have indefinitely felt themselves conscious of — and which they have all tried to sum up in the same WORD. . . .

Because it is the essential manifestation of *that prime fact,* because Pulse *is* Life, therefore it is that we feel Music to be alive when in its pursuit we do act in consonance and harmony with that Supreme Fact . . . and are therefore *in harmony* with NATURE herself!

SUMMARY

THE PRINCIPLES OF TEACHING INTERPRETATION

By TOBIAS MATTHAY

(Report of a Lecture delivered before the Manchester and the Edinburgh Music Teachers' Associations in March, 1910, and before the London Music Teachers' Association in February, 1911, etc. This appeared in *The Music Student* of April, 1911, and is here reprinted verbatim.)

Mr. Matthay remarked that his lecture consisted really of six lectures compressed into one, and it would therefore be of inordinate length. For this reason, also, we can give but a résumé of this lecture.

Six Important Points for Piano Teachers

He said: "The pursuit implied by the term Piano-teaching is so enormously complex, that at first glance it seems hopeless to try to cover the ground in one short discourse. All one can do is to select some of the more salient points where the young teacher (and often the old one also) is apt to fail. It is therefore understood that no attempt is here made to deal exhaustively with the subject. I have selected the following points: (1) the difference between Practice and mere Strumming; (2) the difference between Teaching and Cramming; (3) how the pupil's mind can be brought upon his work; (4) correct ideas of Time and Shape; (5) the element of Rubato; and (6) the element of Duration and Pedalling."

What is Good Teaching?

Mr. Matthay continued, that it would be impossible to make clear even these particular essentials of teaching, without first taking a preliminary, cursory glance at the whole problem of teaching. To begin with, we could not, accurately speaking, "teach" anyone anything, in the sense of being able directly to lodge any knowledge of ours in another mind. One could only stimulate another mind to *wish to learn*, and place before that other mind the things desirable to be learnt. We cannot teach others, but we can help them to learn.

Here we come at once to one of the special points to be discussed, the difference between good teaching and bad teaching, viz., that good teaching consists not in trying to make the pupil "do things" so that it may seem like playing, but in trying to make him *think*, so that it may really be playing. In the first place we try to turn out an automaton, but in the second case we prompt the pupil to be a living intelligent being.

Pupils usually do not realise that it is they who have to make the effort to learn; hence that is the first thing to make plain to them. True, there are "direct" and empiric methods of teaching, but such directness can only refer to *the method of placing things before a pupil*. Work is often brought back worse than at the preceding lesson, owing to practice having been purely automatic. Often this is the pupil's fault, but more often still, the teacher's, owing to his not having shown the pupil how to apply his brains during practice.

The Necessity of Attention

Practice should not consist in trying to "make the piece go better," but in trying to make oneself *see* it better —

understand it better musically and technically. This implies a constant process of analysis during practice, musical analysis and technical analysis. This means we must really listen, both outwardly and inwardly. Nothing is more fatal musically than omitting to do this.

To try to draw without looking at the paper is no worse than trying to play without careful aural attention. This is where "Ear-Training" comes in. But Ear-Training should always mean *training the mind to observe* and analyse Pitch and Time so as to understand Music better, and should never be conducted without that immediate purpose in view. There can be no real practice, nor real lesson, without insistence all the time on such *real* Ear-Training. All this implies the closest possible attention during the practice-hour. Such close attention, in conjunction with a keen imagination, is the distinguishing feature between the work of the talented and un-talented person. One can therefore raise one's status, musically, simply by insisting on close attention to what one is doing, and more important still, to what one *should be doing*, musically and technically.

Such persistent use of the judgement and imagination is not only required from the pupil, but also from the teacher. As teachers, our powers must be applied, analytically, in a two-fold direction. *Firstly*, we must analyse the music we wish to teach, its Structure and its Feeling; and, *secondly*, we must analyse the pupil's doings, comparing them to this ideal we have formed, so that we can diagnose exactly where the pupil fails, and why he fails. Such analysis comes under *four* headings: (*a*) we must analyse *what* the pupil is actually doing; (*b*) we must analyse the faults thereby perceived; (*c*) we must analyse *why* the pupil is making those faults; and (4) we must analyse the pupil's attitude of mind, so that we may know how to treat him.

The Use and Misuse of Example

The lecturer here took these matters in detail. He then pointed out that teachers must learn to explain every point, and must besides educate themselves as musicians and as actual performers, so as to be able to demonstrate the various points by actual example when necessary. Example, by itself, however, was shown to be useless, as its tendency is here again to turn the pupil into "an automatic ape" — example should always be accompanied by full explanation as to shape and feeling, the *purpose* of the means of expression applied. The opening bars of Schumann's *Warum* were here played, and it was shown how an inexperienced pupil would turn this into a laughable parody unless such explanations were given.

Enthusiasm

Allusion was then made to the necessity for enthusiasm, for unless the teacher could all the time show himself really interested in his work, he could not expect his pupils to give the truly exhausting attention required if really good work was to be accomplished. And enthusiasm would grow in us, if we but tried our best all the time. Enthusiasm, however, would not suffice by itself. The teacher must not only be willing to help, but must know *how* to do so, otherwise his work would after all prove a failure.

Cramming v. the Cultivation of Judgement and of Imagination

Mr. Matthay next considered the radical distinction between *useful* teaching and *useless* teaching.

The *wrong* attitude is, to try to make the pupil directly imitate the musical effects, the "points," etc., which your musical sense tells you are required, but without explaining the *why* and *wherefore* musically.   Thus you turn your pupil into a mere responsive automaton, a Trilby to your Svengalism.   This is sheer "cramming," and can have no abiding influence educationally.

The *right* attitude is to insist on your pupil trying to see for himself all the time, to the best of his capacity, musically and technically.   You must *force* him to use his own judgement and imagination, so that that may prompt him all the time; and you must guide that judgement and imagination all the time, so that right seeing and thinking is learnt.

In the first case you teach your pupil to play without thinking, whereas in the second case you teach him to play *because* he is thinking, and is thinking rightly.

Two Main Points — "Key-Resistance" and the "Time-Spot"

To bring your pupil's mind on his work, you must insist on two main points.   You must teach him to attend, in the first place, to "Key-resistance," and, in the second place, to "Time-spot," and by this means you ensure *musical* attention — attention to musical shape and feeling.

By attention to key-resistance is meant a constant attention to the obstruction the key offers before and *during* its descent.   As this resistance varies with every difference in the tone you are making, you can thus judge (and by this means only) what force to apply, so that you may obtain the tone *musically* desired.

By attention to "Time-spot" is meant that you must realise that all music implies Progression, and you must use your inward ear and your outer physical ear to determine *where* in the musical progression each and every sound is precisely due.   You must make clear to the pupil that sounds have no musical significance whatever unless they are made to suggest Progression: there must always be a

sense of Progression, or *movement towards definite landmarks*
— a growth with a definite purpose, a rhythmical and
emotional purpose. This principle of progression applies
equally to the smallest segments of music, and to the largest;
— it applies whether we deal with a progression merely of
three notes, or a complete phrase, or a whole movement. No
child should ever be allowed to touch the piano without being
at once shown how this principle of *progression onwards,
towards cadences*, etc., applies everywhere. Mr. Matthay
illustrated all these points and went into a mass of detail; he
also said that he had pointed out the importance of this
idea of *progression* and "scanning" of the music during the
last 20 years of his teaching life, and in his *First Principles*
(Advice to Teachers), but that the passage was often passed
by, without its being realised that it applies during every
minute of one's teaching life. He pointed out, further,
that only by strict attention to this principle of progression
could one ensure the correction of "sloppiness" in passage-
work, and learn to play the notes in between the pulses
accurately and musically.

   This matter was illustrated, as also the fact that octave
passages, etc., divided between the two hands, still depended
on the same mental principle; unless indeed, the student
had not learnt the right ways of Technique, had not mastered the "Act of Resting," when he would here fail owing
to his being unable to express himself properly. It was
pointed out that to keep this principle of progression in view
while playing a long extended movement is indeed the hardest task a player has to deal with; and that success here
depends, mainly, on an accurate *memory* of the proportionate
importance of all the component progressions of the piece;
and upon a constant self-control in executing the musical
picture thus to be realised as a perfect whole.

Continuity and Rubato

Mr. Matthay then showed, that to enable one to render a piece *continuous* in performance, the *tempo* must be continuous, although it also depended on a correct laying out of tone-values and of the emotional stress. "Remember," he said, "a new Tempo means a new piece — a new train of thought, and that each change of Tempo needs a new adjustment of the listener's attention. Constantly recurring ritardos, and accellerandos, unless on a large scale, are therefore fatal to Continuity. But we cannot express ourselves adequately without Time-*inflections*, hence the necessity of *Rubato*." Rubato was shown to be requisite in all music, although some of the ·older masters required it less than do our modern composers. Rubato should be taught even to children — real Rubato, not playing out of time.

The illustrations of Rubato were specially chosen to prove their necessity even in Beethoven and Bach, although Rubato requires subtle application in these masters. Rubato might extend over a few notes only, or over whole phrases. Rubato was shown to be of two distinct kinds: (*a*) where, for the sake of emphasising a note or several notes, we delay the time, and must then make good the time by hastening the subsequent notes so as to return to the pulse at the crisis of the phrase, etc.; and (*b*) where, for the sake of the *agitato* effect, we begin by hastening the phrase, and must then delay the subsequent notes so as to bring us back again to the pulse at the chief syllable of the phrase — near its end. These two forms can be combined even during the course of a single phrase, and often are. In all cases it is of primary importance to determine exactly *where* we must return to the pulse, and also to determine the *cause* of the Rubato — whether caused in the first instance by a retardation or by an accelleration. The actual degree and curve of the Time-swerve must, however, be left to the fancy of the moment, and the effects must never be applied so as to become noticeable *as such*. These points were made clear by the lecturer by means of short excerpts, showing, for instance, how impossible a Chopin Nocturne would be without Rubato.

The next point, likewise brought home by examples, was to prove how a Rubato would serve to make clear the climax of a phrase in spite of a diminuendo. It was pointed out that the most striking emphasis we can give to any note is its coincidence with the pulse after that has been swerved from during a Rubato.

It was also shown, by examples from Chopin, etc., how Rubato is required to depict agitated feelings — whereas, to give the effect of decision, calmness, truculence, etc., we must avoid Rubato for the moment.

In passages consisting of notes of contrasting length, the tendency should be to emphasise these differences by giving proportionately more time to the longer notes and less to the shorter ones; and incidentally we should find that the same rule applies with regard to *tone*-variety, the tone varying somewhat in accordance with the length of the notes.

A somewhat related tonal effect is required when we continue a phrase after a long note or rest — we must re-start the continuation with far less tone than was given to the last long note, otherwise we should have the effect of a new phrase there.

Tone Contrasts

Mr. Matthay, after exemplifying this, said the importance of Rubato does not minimise the importance of Tone-contrasts and contrasts of Duration; but the absence of both these last is also often overlooked by the teacher. Although made miserable by their absence in the pupils' performances, the teacher, owing to his not noticing the real reason of his discomfort failed to make the slight effort necessary to remedy these things. Most of the failure does not arise from paucity of tone, but from the absence of low tints. Most students, in fact, never get near a *pianissimo*, and accompaniments are always played far too loudly; this was exemplified by a few bars from the opening of the "*Moonlight*" Sonata, it being pointed out that the difference between the good and evil rendering was attributable solely to the "cutting away" of tone in the first instance. Students also invariably played the beginnings of phrases far too high up in tone, hence their failure to show the climaxes.

With regard to the actual teaching of the wherewithal of tone-contrasts — the teaching of Touch, the rationale of the processes of producing Tone, Duration and Agility, there could of course be no teaching worthy the name unless these things were all the time most fully explained and made clear to the pupil. Even Germany, where instruction in these matters had been so hideously bad, even Germany was now waking up to these requirements of the present day.

Pedalling

The lecturer then went on to the subject of Pedalling, which he said was mostly so badly overlooked that even artists' performances were often no better than a child's daubs. It was pitiable to see the amount of care sometimes bestowed on making the fingers execute good phrasing, duration and colouring, when in the meantime the whole effect was wiped out by the right foot. The fault could in most cases be again traced to sheer non-attention to the

actual sounds coming from the piano — playing being too
often regarded as a mere muscular exercise instead of the
making of musical sounds for a musical purpose.

Mr. Matthay here demonstrated the striking contrasts
to be obtained merely by varying the duration of sounds;
and pointed out, as to the details of pedalling, that we have
to learn to syncopate the pedal in legato and in legatissimo,
and further to learn the value of incomplete tenuti, emphasis by the cutting short of a sustained effect at a pulse, and
half-pedalling effects, all of which matters received full illustration. This matter was summed up by saying that we
must always remember that music depends not only on our
fingers but also on our right foot.

Sincere Art

In his peroration, Mr. Matthay indicated how Musical
Art was always on the wrong path unless it was employed
to depict things felt and experienced. To be sincere, Art
must always be used for the purpose of expressing Mood or
Feeling. But it did not follow that by making this endeavour we should succeed, although we should be working
in the right direction. Also, there was the question as to
the appropriateness of the moods chosen to be expressed.
Mr. Matthay then tried to show that in the true basis of
Music — Pulse, Rhythm, Progression — we could find the
reason of its great power over the emotions, this basis
bringing it into intimate union with all the vital manifestations of Nature, and with the ultimate hidden facts of the
Universe and Infinitude itself.

TOBIAS MATTHAY:

PUBLISHED

PIANOFORTE MUSIC.

Four Novelletten—Op. 1	(Forsyth Bros.)	8/- complete
Nocturne in D flat—Op. 3 (new edition)	(Edwin Ashdown)	4/-
Hommage à Chopin—Op. 4 . . .	(Forsyth Bros.)	4/-
Seventeen Variations—Op. 5 . . .	(Forsyth Bros.)	4/-
An Autumn Song—Op. 6 . . .	(Forsyth Bros.)	3/-
In Spring Time (Three Miniatures) Op. 7	(Forsyth Bros.)	5/- complete
A Summer Day Dream—Op. 8 . .	(Forsyth Bros.)	3/6
A Waltz Whim—Op. 9	(Ascherberg)	4/-
In Winter—Op. 10	(Ascherberg)	4/-
Moods of a Moment (ten numbers)—Op. 11	(Ascherberg)	} 7/6 complete 2/6 separate
Love-phases (Minnelieder) (three numbers) Op. 12 (new edition) . . .	(Joseph Williams)	} complete 2/6 nett
Monothemes (six numbers)—Op. 13 .	(Forsyth Bros.)	2/6 nett
Lyrics—Op. 14 (seven numbers) . . .	(Paterson)	2/- nett
Scottish Dances—Op. 15 (four numbers) .	(Paterson)	4/-
Prelude from Suite of Studies—Op. 16 .	(Weekes & Co.)	4/-
Intermezzo in E, from Suite of Studies— Op. 16	(Ricordi)	1/6 nett
Bravura (Finale), from Suite of Studies— Op. 16	(Ricordi)	2/- nett
Elves—Op. 17 (new edition) . . .	(Weekes & Co.)	4/-
Con Imitazione—Op. 18	(Weekes & Co.)	4/-
Romanesque—Op. 19	(Weekes & Co.)	4/-
Toccata—Op. 21 (Avison Edition) . .	(Novello)	3/-
Dirge, from Stray Fancies—Op. 22 (Avison Edition)	(Novello)	2/-
Albumblatt, from Stray Fancies—Op. 22 (Avison Edition)	(Novello)	2/6

FOR PIANOFORTE AND VIOLIN

A Pamphlet—Op. 2.	(Edition Chanot)	4/-

FOR PIANOFORTE AND STRINGS

Quartet in one movement—Op. 20 (Avison Edition)	(Novello)	4/- nett

FOR PIANOFORTE AND ORCHESTRA

Concert-piece, No. 1 in A minor (Concerto in one movement)—Op. 23	(Ricordi)	
Solo, with orchestral accompaniments arranged for a 2d pianoforte		5/- nett
String parts		each: 1/- nett

MS. Full score and wind parts, etc., on hire from publishers.

EDUCATIONAL WORKS FOR PIANOFORTE BY
TOBIAS MATTHAY

With 22 Illustrations. 8vo. pp. xlii + 328. 7s. 6d.
THE ACT OF TOUCH
IN ALL ITS DIVERSITY.
Part I.   Introductory. The Problems of Pianoforte Education.
Part II. The Instrumental Aspect of Key-Treatment.
Part III. The Muscular Aspect of Key-Treatment.
Part IV. On Position.
LONGMANS, GREEN & CO.; 39, Paternoster Row, London, E. C.

Crown 8vo.   2s. 6d.
THE FIRST PRINCIPLES OF PIANOFORTE PLAYING
Being an extract from the Author's "THE ACT OF TOUCH."
Designed for School use, and with two new chapters:
DIRECTIONS FOR LEARNERS AND ADVICE TO TEACHERS.
LONGMANS, GREEN & CO.

Crown 8vo.   1s. 6d.
COMMENTARIES
ON THE TEACHING OF PIANOFORTE TECHNIQUE.
A SUPPLEMENT TO "THE ACT OF TOUCH" AND "FIRST PRINCIPLES."
LONGMANS, GREEN & CO.

Quarto.   6s.
RELAXATION STUDIES
In the Muscular Discriminations required for Touch, Agility and Expression in Pianoforte Playing.
Cloth bound (150 pages, 4to), with numerous illustrations and musical examples;
with a portrait of the Author.
BOSWORTH & CO; Tenterden Street, Hanover Square, London, W.

Quarto.   1s.
THE PRINCIPLES OF FINGERING, LAWS OF PEDALLING, &c.
An Extract from above.
BOSWORTH & CO.

Quarto, with illustrations.   1s. 6d. net, cash.
THE ROTATION PRINCIPLE
ITS APPLICATION AND MASTERY.
Sole Agents for Great Britain and Colonies: JOSEPH WILLIAMS; 32, Great Portland St., London, W.
Sole Agents for U. S. A.· THE BOSTON MUSIC CO. (SCHIRMER); 26 West Street, Boston, Mass.

Quarto, with illustrations.   1s. 6d. net, cash.
THE CHILD'S FIRST STEPS IN PIANO PLAYING
Sole Agents for Great Britain and Colonies: JOSEPH WILLIAMS; 32, Great Portland St., London, W.
Sole Agents for U. S. A.: THE BOSTON MUSIC CO. (SCHIRMER); 26 West Street, Boston, Mass.

Practice Card, No. 1.   1s. net, cash.
DOUBLE–THIRD SCALES
THEIR FINGERING AND PRACTICE.
Sole Agents for Great Britain and Colonies: JOSEPH WILLIAMS; 32, Great Portland St., London, W.
Sole Agents for U S. A.: ARTHUR P. SCHMIDT; 120 Boylston Street, Boston, Mass.

Crown 8vo, with illustrations.   5s. net.
MUSICAL INTERPRETATION
Its laws and principles, and their application in TEACHING AND PERFORMING.
Sole Agents for Great Britain and Colonies: JOSEPH WILLIAMS; 32, Great Portland St., London, W.
Sole Agents for U. S. A.: THE BOSTON MUSIC CO. (Schirmer); 26–28 West Street, Boston, Mass.